COVID-19 *and* Pain

COVID-19 *and* Pain

Can We Still Believe in God?

PETER HARRIS

RESOURCE *Publications* • Eugene, Oregon

COVID-19 AND PAIN
Can We Still Believe in God?

Copyright © 2022 Peter Harris. All rights reserved. Except for brief quotations in critical publications or reviews, no part of this book may be reproduced in any manner without prior written permission from the publisher. Write: Permissions, Wipf and Stock Publishers, 199 W. 8th Ave., Suite 3, Eugene, OR 97401.

Resource Publications
An Imprint of Wipf and Stock Publishers
199 W. 8th Ave., Suite 3
Eugene, OR 97401

www.wipfandstock.com

PAPERBACK ISBN: 978-1-6667-4328-9
HARDCOVER ISBN: 978-1-6667-4329-6
EBOOK ISBN: 978-1-6667-4330-2

APRIL 27, 2022 9:51 AM

Scripture taken from the New Revised Standard Version. Copyright © 1995 by Oxford University Press. Used by permission. All rights reserved.

For the ministers, officers and congregation of my parish church of St Aidan's Gravesend who have, like thousands of other churches globally, maintained faithfully the witness of God's love in the midst of the pandemic.

For Bishop Lusa Nsenga-Ngoy who welcomed me with great warmth back into the Anglican Communion.

And also, for Reverend Jane Winter, for her wisdom.

Contents

Preface | ix
Acknowledgments | xi
Abbreviations | xii
Introduction | xv

The Judicial | 1
The Practical | 9
The Scientific | 22
The Philosophical | 33
The Pastoral | 51
Conclusion | 65

Bibliography | 69

Preface

FOR TWO DAYS I had suffered from a very runny nose and feelings of fatigue, muscle aches, and shivers. I had a productive cough rather than a dry cough and my taste and smell had not disappeared. I did not suspect I had been infected with one of the variants of COVID-19. On the second day I lost my senses of taste and smell. That day was a Tuesday, one of the two days each week that my employer asks me to test myself. Whenever I had tested myself before, only one red line appeared in the test which meant I was virus-free. On this occasion, two red lines manifested. I could not believe it! I performed the test another two times just to be sure, but on each occasion the two, tell-tale, red lines stubbornly appeared to confirm that I was one among the millions of people who have been, are and will be infected. My PCR test also said I was positive. Ten days of self-isolation, much sleeping, and drinking plenty of orange juice lay ahead of me.

I was lucky. Apart from the loss of taste and smell, my symptoms were akin to a nasty head cold. My immune system prevailed quickly and I am back at work. Of course, many people with COVID-19 have been hospitalized and many of them have died. There is also the phenomenon called 'Long Covid' which has left people who have recovered from COVID-19 in a chronically fatigued state. Yes, I am indeed lucky.

My encounter with COVID-19 has prompted me to write about it and as I am a Christian, to try to make sense of it from a Christian perspective. However, when COVID-19 first broke into

Preface

global consciousness back in early 2020, it did not occur to me that I might write a book in response. Some Christian writers did take the opportunity to write early on about the pandemic.[1] I suppose there is within me a desire not to 'condescend' to write about what everyone else is writing about for fear of being seen to be following the crowd. If that is arrogance, then I repent.

But having said that, I think there is an advantage to having waited until this later stage of the pandemic. We have a much better understanding now of the virus and what it has done to individuals, families, communities, and nations. We have also seen how medical science has responded to the pandemic, in particular, producing vaccines very quickly and how other institutions and individuals have played a heroic part in mitigating the suffering involved. With such knowledge available, it is possible to write with greater understanding in order to argue that not only can Christians continue to believe in God despite the suffering they and others are experiencing, but that their worldview provides them with an extraordinarily high view of the value of humans which is fundamental to a robust response to humanitarian crises and whose fundamental suppositions are the origin of the modern science and hospitals used to fight the pandemic. When enduring pain, Christians also have the magnificent hope of everlasting life with God. These are this book's arguments and hopefully ones that by the end of his/her reading, the reader will share.

---

1. See, for example, Lennox, *Where is God in A Coronavirus World?* and Wright, *God and the Pandemic*.

Acknowledgments

MANY THANKS GO TO Dr Jana Harmon for her encouragement to regard the Christian faith as the outcome of reason and for giving me the opportunity to give my testimony on her *Side B Podcast*. Many thanks go also to Dr Harry Edwards who has provided me with many opportunities to publish articles on apologetics. It is their and others' encouragement that has helped motivate me to continue as an apologist.

Abbreviations

AD: *Anno Domini*, or those years after Christ's birth, which is taken to be the year 0.

AIDS: Acquired Immunity Deficiency Syndrome.

BBC: British Broadcasting Company.

BC: Those years before Christ's birth, which is taken to be the year 0.

C: When preceding a date, it means approximately, as the exact date is unknown.

1 Cor: First epistle to the Corinthians.

COVID-19: Coronavirus disease.

DNA: Deoxyribonucleic acid which carries genetic instructions for the growth, development, functioning and reproduction of all organisms.

Eph: Epistle to the Ephesians.

Exod: Book of Exodus.

Flu: Influenza.

Gen: Book of Genesis.

HIV: The human immunodeficiency virus.

Isa: Book of Isaiah

LGBTQ+: An umbrella term that describes a range of sexualities which includes lesbian, gay, bi-sexual, transgender, and queer.

Abbreviations

NHS: National Health Service in Britain.

Op: *Opus* or a work such as a book or piece of music.

PCR test: Polymerase chain reaction test used to confirm finally that a person has COVID-19.

1 Pet: The apostle Peter's first epistle.

Ps: Psalm.

Rev: Book of Revelation.

Rom: Epistle to the Romans.

UK: United Kingdom.

Vol: Volume (referring to a specific publication within a series).

WHO: World Health Organization.

Introduction

THE PERENNIAL QUESTION

WHY GOD, WHO IS held to be all-good, all-powerful, and all-knowing, would allow evil (caused by human behavior) and pain (caused by the natural world) is a perennial question not only of philosophers and theologians but one for every person, for all suffer. To those who believe in God or gods, it is a stubbornly problematic question, but they believe there are answers. For those who disbelieve in any God, what they perceive to be the failure to answer the question may well be the decisive problem that supports their unbelief. For agnostics, the problems of evil and pain may be a reason for their uncertainty about God's existence. They may find arguments for God's existence persuasive, but cannot reconcile those reasons with the existence of evil and pain; therefore, they withhold judgement. People also suffer to varying degrees and in different ways. Some suffer more than others. Some will bear suffering better than others. There are those who suffer primarily with their health, whereas others are more frequently the victims of things such as political oppression and crime. Some, of course, will face a combination of these pains and evils. Many will face natural disasters and many of them will not survive. All of us at some point will be badly treated by another person. All of us at some point will be bereaved and cause grief when we die too. Suffering evil and pain is the consequence of morally wrong behavior, living in a world of natural dangers and disasters, and the death that comes to us all.

INTRODUCTION

THE PANDEMIC

The COVID-19 pandemic is an example of pain. It is a member of the set of pains which contains such things as terminal illnesses and the destruction wrought by earthquakes and tsunamis. Sometimes pain is the consequence only of natural events. The people who die in an earthquake have suffered at the hands of a purely natural force in which no human agency was involved. Sometimes natural events combine with evil human behavior to cause pain. Deforestation, caused by humans' greedy desire for maximum profit from timber wood, is a cause of desertification, which in turn puts human lives (and that of animals and plants) at risk. Here it is evil that initiates pain. It has been hypothesized that COVID-19 was accidentally leaked from a scientific laboratory in Wuhan, but the evidence appears to point to zoonosis or the transference of the virus from bats or pangolins to humans.[1] COVID-19 is likely therefore to be in its origin a pain, however, it has caused evil in turn, such as selfish panic buying and the hoarding of food and other resources.

COVID-19 may be a new virus, but it is not a new form of pain. If we look back into history, we see that pandemics have been a frequent, universal human experience. Probably the oldest recorded pandemic comes from the Roman Empire. It is known as the Antonine Plague and it killed around five million people between AD 165–80.[2] From the historical sources that describe the symptoms, historians of disease believe it was an outbreak of measles or smallpox.[3] Perhaps the most well-known pandemic has come to be known as the Black Death which was the bubonic plague that swept across Eurasia in 14th century, reducing the world's population by a fifth.[4] The 'Spanish Flu' took, it is estimated, between twenty million and fifty million lives (1918–1920).[5] In more recent

---

1. Andersen et al, 'The proximal origin of SARS-CoV-2', 450–452.
2. Lennox, *Where is God in a Coronavirus World?* 10.
3. Lennox, *Where is God in a Coronavirus World?* 10.
4. Lennox, *Where is God in a Coronavirus World?*, 10.
5. Lennox, *Where is God in a Coronavirus World?*, 10.

INTRODUCTION

times, 'Asian Flu' (1956–58), killed two million, 'Hong Kong Flu' (1968–1969) killed a further one million and HIV/AIDS, which continues to this day, has accounted for the deaths of thirty-two million people.[6] These are the worst known pandemics and yet our ancestors lived with regular occurrences of fast-spreading disease until public health policies and vaccinations prevented them and medical treatments cured them.

The COVID-19 pandemic is therefore not unique in its extent and the pain it causes. At the present moment of writing. according to the WHO's statistics, on 18 March 2022, 6,062,536 people have died from the virus.[7] In terms of sheer numbers of dead, COVID-19 has been deadlier than either the Asia or Hong Kong Flu, but yet has not managed to equal the Spanish Flu or HIV/AIDS and hopefully will not. However, when one considers that of all COVID-19 cases, only around 1.3 percent of patients have died,[8] the pandemic's relative lethality is low, though the numbers that have died is high because 464,809,377 people have contracted it,[9] due to its rapid transmissibility, the fact that many people do not develop symptoms and therefore unwittingly pass it on, and the ease and frequency of national and global travel.

If pandemics are not original, though the Media sometimes like to report them as if they were, neither are the public health measures taken to prevent its spread. Washing hands, wearing masks, and maintaining a physical distance from other people were methods used to slow the spread of Spanish Flu. Quarantining infected people and locking down cities were methods used during the Middle Ages.

Even COVID-19's rapid transmissibility is not novel. The fourteenth century bubonic plague, or the Black Death as it is also known, could be contracted by simply touching an item that an infected victim had touched. Such speed of infection caught

---

6. Lennox, *Where is God in a Coronavirus World?*, 10.
7. WHO, "Coronavirus (COVID-19) Dashboard,"
8. WHO, "Coronavirus (COVID-19) Dashboard."
9. WHO, "Coronavirus (COVID-19) Dashboard."

medieval societies off-guard whose methods of warning others of the coming infection were much less rapid than ours.

I would suggest though that there are two things that are novel about this pandemic. First, the virus is a new one, even though it is categorized within the group of coronaviruses that causes colds, influenza, and pneumonia. With that fact comes a lot of uncertainty for epidemiologists trying to understand its behavior and that of the inevitable mutations. Second, national lockdowns have been necessary, of which no one has had previous experience. Whole populations have been told to take refuge in their homes and work from home with the exception of key workers whose services are necessary to the economy's functioning and the provision of healthcare. Trips outside the home have been limited to those deemed necessary such as shopping. Mass electronic communication has enabled whole nations of many millions of people to coordinate their response in ways that ancient, medieval, and early modern societies would have found impossible to do. Those living with poor health, or who are dying, need no reminders of their finitude. The total response of national lockdown has also reminded those whose health is good, and whose lives are more or less free of significant suffering, that they too are flesh and bone and will eventually return to the dust. Shades, indeed more than shades, of mortality.

National lockdowns can be a necessary yet brutal medicine. People lose their jobs through economic inactivity despite the furlough schemes that governments that are rich enough have put in place. The sense of isolation felt by people is deleterious to mental health and has increased the suicide rate. People who would normally seek medical treatment have not done so for fear of catching COVID-19 in hospital. Deaths from conditions other than COVID-19 have therefore spiked. National health services now have an enormous backlog of non-emergency surgical operations to perform. Health and care workers report high levels of exhaustion and trauma. The victims of COVID-19 and the national responses it has provoked therefore consist of a much wider group than those who have been infected and those who have died. The scale of pain has been monumental and has augmented the levels of pain that go on every day anyway in the lives of all humans. Surely in the face of all this we ought to jettison our belief in God or the gods and join the ranks of the atheists or the agnostics?

THE CHRISTIAN PERSPECTIVE

I wish to tackle this question from a Christian perspective and suggest ways in which the apparent contradiction between the Christian God of love and COVID-19's pain can be made more tractable and therefore open to some measure of resolution. My aim is modest because of my desire not to promise more than I can deliver, for despite my confidence that Christianity is a robust worldview in the face of the problem of suffering, there is much mystery that clings to the subject which I do not believe can be resolved in this life and with our finite minds. Some might say I am playing the 'mystery card', but that is not true because where there is clarity I am very willing to assert it. I want the mystery to be cleared up, not perpetuated. Having said that, there is a genuine mystery to the subject because we are dealing with a God who is ultimately beyond our finite conceptualizations. We do our best, therefore, treading carefully and understanding what we can.

When people are experiencing or witnessing great pain, their primary desire is that it stops. In the midst of suffering, God can seem distant and silent to those who believe in him. After the death of his wife, Joy Davidman (1915–1960), C. S. Lewis (1898–1963) wrote that when we are happy, God seems present and accessible and yet when we are suffering, he seems distant and behind a trenchantly locked door.[10] I do not think this is always the case. I can think of moments in my life when I have suffered and God has felt close, as if he were standing next to me. I can think also of times when God has seemed absent during painful episodes. To be honest, I do not have an explanation of which I am certain to explain why God felt present and also absent in various pains. For those

10. Lewis, A Grief Observed, 7.

INTRODUCTION

who do not believe God exists, or are uncertain of his existence, their pain reinforces their disbelief and doubt. What sort of God, if he exists, would create a world and then stand aside and watch millions of people struggling in their pain? Could he not have prevented this, or at least do something about it? Such questions can be asked by believer, agnostic, and unbeliever alike. It does not help when prominent Christian leaders assert the erroneous view that COVID-19 could be, or is God's judgment. It is therefore important to reassure people that God is on their side and many Christians have been and are pivotal in preventing, mitigating and resolving suffering. To use the cliché: they put their money where their mouth is, or at least many do.

Chapter 1's task is therefore to demonstrate why COVID-19 is not God's judgment and that instead Christians ought to see CO-VID-19 as the consequence of human failures. Chapter 2 takes a practical angle by asserting that Christianity's moral codes dispose its adherents to selfless and effective responses to pain and that the historical and contemporary data reveal how this has been and is the case. God reaches to people in their pain through his people on earth. It is partly for this reason that the universal church is called the Body of Christ. Chapter 3 looks at Christianity and science because it is science that is in the frontline in the fight against COVID-19. It argues that Christianity has nurtured science historically and was the cultural soil from which modern science and therefore modern medicine emerged. Chapter 4 is the philosophical part which looks to resolve to some extent the contradiction of the belief in God with the fact of COVID-19. Its central argument is that pain is the consequence of human free will, but that free will is what makes having a relationship of love with God possible. Chapter 5 has a pastoral aim for it examines what grief feels like and then describes the Good News of the Christian message which is the context of hope for all, both humans and the natural world. My final chapter draws all these lines of thought into a summation and an acknowledgement of the enduring mystery of these issues.

INTRODUCTION

OTHER WORLDVIEWS

In arguing for the distinctiveness of the Christian approach to suffering, I do not wish to denigrate other worldviews. This is partly because I do not know enough about, let us say, the Buddhist or the Islamic approach to the problems of evil and pain; it is also partly due to the fact that in facing suffering such as pandemics, global cooperation is required between people of different religions and none. People of all faiths and none have died in this pandemic and their relatives have been unable to be with them as they were dying due to the quarantining of patients. A Hindu grieves for the loss of a parent as much as an atheist, an agnostic, and a Christian. Our desire to defeat this virus is what unites us and therefore to argue for the supremacy of the Christian world view would be rather tactless. Moreover, I wish to acknowledge the beneficial influence of Judaism on Christianity with respect to its understanding and response to suffering through the use of portions from the sacred Hebrew texts. This ought not to be controversial to Christian readers since the Jewish Scriptures (known to Christians as the Old Testament) are regarded as divinely breathed by Christianity and contain within them an enormous range of wise reflection on suffering.

Nevertheless, in the course of my arguments I shall challenge the more extreme kinds of atheists, particularly those who fight under the banner of New Atheism,[11] whose opinions of Christianity as an evil moral system and hostile to science have been the most infamous intellectual assault on Christianity in the past twenty years, if not more. Their views need to be challenged if I am to make my case. Though their public prominence has waned,[12] their beliefs continue to circulate and affect many people's attitudes. Therefore, I wish to refute them within the context of my discussion of the pandemic, though they are not my focus. Having said

---

11. The de facto leaders of New Atheism are the evolutionary biologist Richard Dawkins, the journalist Christopher Hitchens (1949–2011), the writer Sam Harris and the philosopher Daniel Dennett.

12. Bruenig, "Is the New Atheism Dead?" See also Poole, "The Four Horsemen review" and Lamb, 'The delusions of New Atheism.'

INTRODUCTION

this, I wish to assure the reader that I do not view all atheists in the same light and acknowledge the measured criticisms of Christianity by intelligent atheists such as Michael Ruse and John Gray and the appreciation of Christianity's benignity by intelligent atheists and agnostics such as Camille Paglia, Tom Holland, and Douglas Murray. Moreover, though I refrain from criticizing directly other religious worldviews, I do wish to exhibit the cogency and goodness of the Christian worldview and assert that it has provided us with a very robust means of dealing with the current crisis. With these reassurances in place, it is time now to consider the question of whether the COVID-19 pandemic is God's punishment.

The Judicial

COVID-19 IS NOT GOD'S JUDGEMENT

I need to reassure the reader that I do not believe, as some Christians do, that COVID-19 is a plague sent as a judgment by God for people's sins. Whenever a natural disaster strikes, with monotonous predictability there are those within the Christian faith who will say they know certainly that what is happening is God's judgment. Take, for example, the American pastor John Piper who when asked what he would say to those pastors who see the pandemic as God's judgement on sinful nations and cities stated that God sometimes will use disease to judge those who have rejected him and are very sinful.[1] Piper does not say definitely that COVID-19 is God's judgement, but leaves the door open to such a possibility. Other American pastors have been more forthright in their view. Ralph Drollinger thinks the pandemic is God's wrath on the USA because of violations of God's laws.[2] The Christian author William Koenig has opined that COVID-19 is God's judgment of fashion shops and sports teams being pro-LGBTQ+.[3] All the examples I have given are pronouncements by leading American evangelicals, but I do not mean to suggest that it is only leading American evangelicals who are saying such things and I certainly do not mean to say that this is the view of all American evangelicals. My examples

---

1. Merritt, "Failing the Coronavirus Test."
2. Merritt, "Failing the Coronavirus Test."
3. Wakefield, "COVID was God's punishment."

are a consequence of the web-pages I managed to turn up in a moment of lazy research through 'googling' the question "Is COVID-19 God's punishment?" I am sure similar examples can be found across the world in other Christian denominations and in other religions.

I do not doubt for once that God judges people. By the end of the Bible's third chapter, God has judged sin (Gen. 3:17–24) and Revelation 20 provides a description of the Last Judgment. The problem with calling COVID-19 God's judgment is that the way the virus and its variants have harmed humanity presents God as unjust in the eyes of the world. A fundamental criterion of just judgment is that only the guilty are held to account. The people who are most likely to die of COVID-19 are the elderly and the immunocompromised-basically the weakest in our society. Children and babies are also the victims of the virus, though their mortality rate is very low. Those who say the pandemic is God's judgement are claiming that God is targeting the weak, which does not sound like God's justice at all. There is also the question as to why faithful Christians have perished in the pandemic.[4] If COVID-19 is God's judgement, why are they also struck down by it?

Another flaw in the view that COVID-19 is God's judgment is that it prohibits anyone from offering help to the virus' victims, for alleviating the problem surely is resisting God's will? However, many Christians who work in the medical services and charities are working overtime to treat the disease, slow its progress and help those who are suffering the emotional and economic consequences. Are they opposed to God even when their motive is love? Furthermore, were those ancient and medieval Christians who mitigated plagues also in opposition to God's will, even when their selfless care brought many to salvation? It therefore does not make sense to call this modern plague God's judgement and we need to find another way of describing COVID-19.

---

4. For example, according to the Barnabas Fund, Christian leaders in India and Nepal are dying of COVID-19 at such a high rate that Christian ministries and churches are at risk of closing. See Barnabas Fund, "Over 2,000 Covid deaths amongst pastors."

JESUS' TEACHINGS ON JUDGEMENT

How then are we to understand God's judgment? Our means for understanding God's judgement is through the lens of Jesus' teachings in the New Testament. Here is an account from Luke's Gospel in which Jesus teaches about God's judgement with regards to two well-known tragedies of his time:

> "At that very time there were some present who told him [Jesus] about the Galileans whose blood Pilate had mingled with their sacrifices. He asked them, "Do you think that because these Galileans suffered in this way they were worse sinners than all other Galileans? No, I tell you; but unless you repent, you will all perish as they did. Or those eighteen who were killed when the tower of Siloam fell on them—do you think that they were worse offenders than all the others living in Jerusalem? No, I tell you; but unless you repent, you will all perish just as they did" (Luke 13:1–5).

In this text, we see examples of evil and error rather than pain, but Jesus' point applies to pain also. Jesus is informed that Pontius Pilate (died after 36 AD), the Roman governor of Judea, had ordered the murder of Jewish worshippers in the act of sacrificing to God (v.1). The reason for this is not known, though the governor was renowned for his violent methods of keeping control of his Jewish subjects.[5] Jesus, in turn, refers to the collapse of the Siloam tower which killed eighteen people (v. 4), caused by building operations around the tower undertaken to improve Jerusalem's water supply.[6] Both tragedies are the consequence of human actions: in the first instance, violent political repression and in the second, what appears to be error. Rather than agree with the view that catastrophes happen to people because they are worse sinners than the rest, Jesus warns against self-righteousness on the part of his listeners by turning their attention to repenting of their own sin (v. 5). His message is this: do not conclude that other people are

---

5. Reicke, *The New Testament Era*, 190.
6. Porter, "Luke," 1210.

worse sinners than you because you think God has judged them by inflicting devastation, but repent of the sin in your own life. We are therefore not to take a holier-than-thou view of another's suffering. If we despise such people as the worst kind of sinners, our motivation and ability to help them is compromised. Instead, we are to examine our own sins and repent before we face judgement on the Day of Judgement.

Another example of Jesus challenging the assumption that all suffering is God's judgement for sin is found recorded in John 9:1–7:

> "As he [Jesus] walked along, he saw a man blind from birth. His disciples asked him, "Rabbi, who sinned, this man or his parents, that he was born blind?" Jesus answered, "Neither this man nor his parents sinned; he was born blind so that God's works might be revealed in him. We must work the works of him who sent me while it is day; night is coming when no one can work. As long as I am in the world, I am the light of the world." When he had said this, he spat on the ground and made mud with the saliva and spread the mud on the man's eyes, saying to him, "Go, wash in the pool of Siloam" (which means Sent). Then he went and washed and came back able to see."

Here we have an example of pain: a man with congenital blindness. Jesus' disciples ask the question that reflects their cultural assumptions: is this man's blindness a consequence of his or his parents' sin (v. 2)? Jesus' response is that it was neither him nor his parents who caused his blindness. The reason for the man's blindness is so that God's works might be seen (v. 3), which in this case is Jesus' healing him (vv. 6–7).

Jesus' response regarding the question of the cause of the man's blindness enables us to see suffering in a different way. The man's blindness is an example of what theologians call providence. Most Christian theologies do not regard providence as the idea that everything that happens in the world is the consequence of God's will, a view that leaves no room for human free will, but rather the view that despite what happens, God's purposes win through in the end.[7] Part of this divine process is God making use of evil and pain to achieve his purposes. That does not mean that these things are caused by God, but it is within his power to use them for his glory and aims. The man's congenital blindness has been permitted by God so that he might display his goodness by healing him. By demonstrating his goodness, God is able to invite people into everlasting relationship with him who now have a reason to begin to trust him as a good God. The formerly blind man receives the same invitation and he responds affirmatively: He becomes a follower of Jesus. Far greater is the everlasting joy this man has than the temporary distress he has endured as a blind man. Far greater too is the everlasting joy of those who have believed because of the man's healing than the woes into which they too have been born.

GOD'S MEGAPHONE

Has God therefore allowed in his providence COVID-19 that he may display his goodness to the world? I think so, but that is only part of the answer and if we do not give the rest of the answer, we are in danger of making God look foolish, for surely, he could display his goodness without needing to permit suffering? God does not cause suffering: It is the consequence of human free will and the choices all of us have made. We shall explore the argument from free will in greater detail in chapter three. Within the context of human free agency, God uses the evil and pain we cause as a means of getting our attention.[8]

Think of how many things distract us from God. Our lives are taken over by things which are good when kept in proportion, but which have become priorities rather than God: Things such as careers, ambitions, pleasures, and relationships. Pain cuts through all of this because it leads us to ask questions such as why am I in pain and why is there pain in the first place? Once a person asks these

---

7. Tomlin, "Is the coronavirus a judgement from God?"
8. Lewis, *The Problem of Pain*, 81.

questions, s/he is starting to think in a Christian way (though this way of thinking is not unique to Christianity) for s/he has noticed something about existence as such and does not think it is right. It is the beginning of the Christian worldview to conclude that there is something not right about the world and something not right about ourselves. Christianity says the world has fallen from its very good state and human beings are infected with sin. Suffering is the consequence of both but more on this later.

God gets our attention not only through pain, but also through the good things he gives us in response to our pain, whether we acknowledge him or not. Therefore, a fully paid-up member of the British Humanist Society admitted to hospital with COVID-19 is benefitting from an institution which, as we will see, was invented by Christians and therefore is a good from God. The kindness of strangers is a pleasure to receive that ultimately comes from God. When we experience the kindness of strangers, we may end up asking the question, where does such goodness come from? This is one way of understanding Lewis' view that God whispers through our pleasures, though I think God can be much louder than a whisper when he tries to catch our attention in this way. We could attempt to explain it as a form of *quid pro quo*: A is kind to B because A needs B to be kind in return. Yet often we do acts of kindness without any thought of how the recipient of our kindness will respond and we are altruistic to those we know cannot reciprocate. More extremely, people risk their lives to save others and on occasion will lose their lives intentionally for others' sake. In a world we are told is at its most fundamental level about the personal survival of our genes into future generations through procreation, such survival-reducing behaviour seems odd, unless someone risks death, or is killed, in defence of their children who carry their genes. There seems to be another principle at work here and to ask where that principle comes from is to begin to think that there is more to our world than matter arranged around natural selection, random genetic mutation, and the struggle for survival. Once we start to think like this, God is more than whispering to us: He is speaking. He is inviting us to experience directly his perfect goodness as exemplified, albeit it in a circumscribed way, through people.

WHAT KIND OF JUDGEMENT IS COVID-19?

What then ought we to make of the language of judgement found in the Bible? In a fascinating article called 'Is the coronavirus a judgement from God?',[9] Graham Tomlin, the Bishop of Kensington, explores the possible meanings of the Greek work *krisis* which is the word commonly translated into English as judgement in order to help us think anew about God's judgment. *Krisis* can be translated to mean a verdict and a crisis. Tomlin suggests that God's judgment is best understood as his allowing a long-standing situation to come to a head in the form of a crisis which demands decisive action on the part of those responsible for the crisis and those who can help. However, for Tomlin, the situation is more than that. Divine judgement is when events are permitted by God to combine to reveal the full ugliness of the misuse of the world and people's sins with the accompanying obligation that something needs to be done to put these issues right, a process Christians call repentance. Tomlin draws the conclusion that COVID-19 has more to tell us about ourselves than about God. What sort of things does Tomlin have in mind?

First, Tomlin is of the opinion that COVID-19 raises the issue of how humans treat animals. As noted earlier, the virus most likely jumped from animals to humans by those animals eaten by humans. This therefore calls into question how humans manage and sell animals and how they relate to animals, which points to additional sins such as factory farming, the extinction of species caused by economic activity and over-hunting, and the pollution of natural habitats.

Tomlin also theorizes that COVID-19 has reminded people of the vital importance of face-to-face communication. As people have turned to online communication during lockdown, whilst

---

9. Tomlin, "Is the coronavirus a judgement from God?"

that method has been useful, it has become clear that it is no substitute to meeting in person, and if we know the person well enough, the handshake or hug that will be part of that meeting.

Perhaps more seriously, Tomlin describes how the pandemic has drawn our attention to the inequalities within our societies. It is the poor who are most affected by the virus. It is they who live in crowded housing and who have less resilience when they catch the virus because their health is on average already worse than those better off.

Most importantly for Tomlin, COVID-19 is a stark reminder that humans are not in complete control of their environments and personal lives. Technology has created the illusion of control, whereas the virus has faced us with our mortality and grief. We might think we are rulers of the world, but in that we are tragically mistaken.

COVID-19 is therefore an opportunity to reflect on our way of life which we might not have done if the pandemic had not come and made significant changes. I do not think that Tomlin by saying this is denying the terrible loss of human life and the weight of suffering that this has caused to victims of the virus and their families, many of whom could not be with their loved ones as they died. If there is anything good that could come out of this modern plague, it may well be structural and personal reforms born of international, national, corporate, and personal confessions of sin that may preclude enormous amounts of future suffering.

IN SUMMARY

If Covd-19 is not the judgment of God in that God has not struck us with it, but has allowed us to be judged by our own actions, then to change our behaviours whilst also mitigating and overcoming the pandemic is not to frustrate the will of God, but to do his will. It is the purpose of the next chapter to demonstrate how the Christian worldview enables its adherents to be robust in doing God's will in the face of the pandemic and indeed all kinds of suffering.

The Practical

A MORALITY FRAMEWORK AND A TRACK RECORD

WHAT IS IT ABOUT the Christian worldview that makes genuine Christians so responsive to pain and what historical and contemporary data do we have that demonstrates that Christians, because of their worldview, have been in the forefront of pain's alleviation? The moral motivation behind Christian love is the belief that humans are not only valuable, but absolutely valuable because of God's free creation and love of them. It is this behaviour-shaping belief in the absolute value of humans that has led Christians over the centuries and contemporarily to give to civilisations powerful means to alleviate suffering. This track record is far from morally perfect, but Christians do not believe they are morally perfect in this world and ought not to if they do! There is enough in what they have done that is remarkable and it is important to proclaim this to a world that has too often heard the New Atheist nonsense that religion is a poison that ruins everything.

HUMAN VALUE

A person does not have to have a religious faith, or to be a Christian, in order to view humans as valuable. From an agnostic perspective, Immanuel Kant's (1724–1804) assertion that no human should be treated as a means but as an end in him or herself, utilitarianism's principle of the greatest happiness of the greatest number as a measure of an action's moral value, and secular humanism's human rights are philosophies that hold to a high view of humans. From a religious perspective, all religions place the importance of all or some humans at their centre.[1]

The challenge faced by each moral framework is explaining the source of human value. It might appear fairly easy to explain the value of people who are members of our families, friends, good colleagues, and neighbours, but explaining the source of value of strangers and even enemies is a far harder task which requires a level of objective thinking other than the subjective feelings of value we have for those close to us.

Christianity identifies the source of human value within the love of God who is absolute and is the Creator. Humans are as contingent within the Christian worldview as they are from a materialist perspective. Darwinist biology tells us that humans may not have existed at all if the very long chain of human evolution had been broken at any point, something that very easily could have happened. Genetic research suggests that about one million years ago, human populations were low enough to risk extinction.[2] Around 70,000 years ago it is hypothesized that the explosion of a super-volcano nearly wiped humans out.[3] From an atheist perspective, there was no divine will ensuring human survival: It happened fortuitously. From a Christian perspective, God intervened on these and other occasions to ensure the survival of his human creation. Theologically, humans are contingent. I say theologically because it is a doctrine of God that he is completely self-sufficient and therefore does not create because he needs to, for he needs nothing outside of himself. He therefore does not need human love. His decision to create us was a completely free decision in that nothing constrained God to create. He could have done otherwise

---

1. I say 'some' as those religions that have performed human sacrifice, for example, or pursue religious violence, cannot be said to hold all humans as valuable.

2. Storrs, "Endangered Species."

3. Storrs, "Endangered Species."

The Practical

in that he could have created something other than what he did and he could have refrained from creating anything at all. All of creation is therefore contingent upon God's decision to create.

If God was not constrained to make us he nevertheless freely chose to. We are not necessary beings because we could not have existed; we are therefore possible beings. But we are absolute beings in the sense that we were made by God whose decision to make us is irrevocable. We are absolute also in the sense that though God may not have willed us, what God wills never fails to be efficacious. We are valuable because we were meant to be by the greatest being who is God. That is not the whole picture, however.

We were meant to be because God chose to love such ones as us and chose to receive our love in return. For us to love God, we would in some way have to be like him for, he is love (1 John 4:8). This is why God created us in his image.

To be able to love God and each other requires that we possess additional attributes that may also be termed as what it means to be made in God's image. The theologian James Montgomery Boice (1938–2000) puts it like this: We are made in God's image because we have a personality, are morally conscious, and are spiritual in that we can commune with God.[4] God also possesses personality, has complete knowledge of good and evil, and is spirit. Possessing freedom, a personality, a conscience, and a spirit are the essential ingredients of being able to sustain a relationship of love with God.

As God's nature is the moral absolute that underpins all moral values, his conferring of value upon every human being through his love of each is an absolute value of worth. It therefore follows that if every human being is of absolute worth and cannot be reduced to a gene-propagating machine, each individual is worthy of altruistic help, acts of supererogation, and even acts of self-sacrifice. Perhaps now we understand why ancient Christians risked their lives and died helping plague victims whilst the pagan world looked on incredulously.

---

4. Montgomery Boice, *Foundations of the Christian Faith*, 150–1.

CHRISTIANITY'S MORAL FRAMEWORK.

To assign absolute value to all humans is the basis of the Christian moral framework. By the Christian moral framework, I do not mean a single code of ethics to which all Christians have signed up, for there is no such thing. There are significant differences of opinion among Christians as to what is right and wrong. Some Christians are vegetarians and vegans whereas many are content to eat meat and fish and use products derived from animals such as leather. Some Christians believe that it is possible for some wars to be just, whereas others are pacifists and opposed to war under any circumstances. What is at the heart of Christian ethics on which all Christians can agree is Jesus' summation of God's law into two commandments:

> "'... you shall love the Lord your God with all your heart, and with all your soul, and with all your mind, and with all your strength. The second is this: You shall love your neighbour as yourself. There is no other commandment greater than these'" (Mark 12:29-30).

Matthew's Gospel adds that Jesus made this comment when describing these two commandments: "'On these two commandments hang all the Law and Prophets'" (20:40). In other words, these two commandments were the fundamental and summative principles of ethical behaviour first for Jews and then Christians.

It is God's love and loving God from which Christians get their power to love their neighbors as themselves. Like the lawyer in the Gospels who asks Jesus which was the greatest commandment, we might also wish to know who our neighbor is. The word for us has connotations of the people who live near us in our neighbourhood, but Jesus told his famous parable of the good Samaritan to tell us that the idea of a neighbor is much wider than this (Luke 10:29-37). In the story, a man Jesus calls a Samaritan discovers on the infamously dangerous road from Jericho to Jerusalem a man who has been robbed and nearly beaten to death (v. 33). Rather than ignore him like others have done (vv. 31-32),[5] he cleanses

---

5. In the parable Jesus describes how two men who were supposed to be

The Practical

and binds up the man's wounds, takes him to an inn and takes care of him (v. 34). When the Samaritan leaves the next day, he provides the inn keeper with money to continue the victim's treatment with the promise that he will return and pay the inn keeper any money he spends beyond the amount given (v. 35). Jesus completes his story by asking the lawyer who is the neighbor to the beaten man and the lawyer rightly concludes it is the Samaritan (vv. 36–37).

One thing that might make this parable obscure to us is Jesus' description of the man as a Samaritan. We know that the Jewish people who would have heard Jesus' parable detested the Samaritans for they were half-Jews as they had intermarried with other ethnic groups in the area, something that Jews were prohibited from doing, not for racist reasons, but because of cultural reasons, for it was believed that inter-marriage with people who did not worship Israel's God would lead Jewish people away from the true religion. Jesus is challenging his audience's prejudices by casting the Samaritan as the story's hero. This in itself is a demonstration of what it means to love one's neighbour as oneself: We are not to make judgments of people based on stereotypes.

The lawyer's original question is who is our neighbor? Jesus' question asks who is the neighbor to the robbery victim. The answer is the Samaritan. We are all to be like the Samaritan, therefore we are to think of ourselves as the neighbour first who is ready to love others as ourselves. If everyone were to be like the Samaritan, and this is what Jesus is teaching, we would all be good neighbours to one another. The neighbor is therefore not only those who live around us and ourselves who live near them; the neighbor can be anyone we come into contact with and we are the neighbor whom others come into contact with. This is the universal ethic of love that Christianity proposes to a world that desperately needs such love. It is an extraordinarily demanding moral standard which is impossible to achieve consistently, even by Christians who would

---

exemplars of the Jewish faith, a priest and a Levite who helped the priests minister in the Temple, ignored the victim and passed by on the other side of the road, perhaps out of fear that the man was a trap to lure them to where bandits were lying in wait (Luke 10:31–32).

agree that this is what God wants from people, for it requires each one of us to love others and ourselves, things that we struggle to do.

The sort of love asked of us is not necessarily an intimate one and for the most part will not be, for we are intimate with a small number of people and most people we deal with are not intimates. With those we know well, we know how they want to be loved and we can choose carefully and accurately how to love them. With those we know less well and not at all, the principle Jesus is commanding is to think about how we would like to be treated by them. It is a rule of thumb that can be applied until we know that person better. Therefore, if I were carrying my baby on to a train and had lots of luggage also, I would like someone to give up their seat for me; therefore, if I see someone boarding a train with a baby and much luggage, I would give up my seat. That is how I can love someone I do not know. My love might also be self-sacrificial in that I might be feeling tired and reluctant to give up my seat; but I would still give up my seat because the parent and baby need the seat more than I do. The parent might refuse my offer out of love for me, and a sort of negotiation would then ensue as to who will be doing whom the favour, but we have acted out of love towards each other.

Saying that people, including ourselves, deserve such grand love makes sense when we remember that the first thing Christianity teaches about human beings is that they are God's creations and are made in his image. This gives humans an inherent dignity and value since they are loved by an infinite and everlasting God who is the ultimate standard of goodness. God is the absolute and insuperable reference point for the value of humans. This does not guarantee that people will treat each other lovingly. Far from it. Take for instance the Thirty Years' War (1618–48) that was fought between Catholics and Protestant forces. Both sides possessed a theology that placed the highest possible value on human beings and yet that did not prevent the conflict which killed 20 percent of the German population. It is also tragic that the two World Wars began in Europe, one of the ancient homelands of Christianity. The

The Practical

causes of these wars were not religious but secular such as national security, nationalism, and imperial expansion, and yet Christianity's influence on the civilizations that fought these Wars was unable to prevent the shocking violence of total war. Christianity is not a magic solution that ensures peace. However, when the divine value of humans affects belief and behaviour, remarkable things are achieved. It is reasonably argued the notion of human rights can be traced back to eleventh century Catholic canon law,[6] a concept that has survived to have a global reach, thanks to the United Nations Universal Declaration of Human Rights in 1948 which was in part a moral response to the Nazi genocides and atrocities in conquered territories.[7] Human rights are a human invention under the influence of Christianity and perpetuated by secular humanism, though without the metaphysical underpinnings of belief in God. Time will tell if their godless, secular experiment will work. I cannot say I am optimistic.

PUTTING THEIR MONEY WHERE THEIR MOUTHS ARE

Before Christianity was made the official religion of ancient Rome by Emperor Constantine (AD 272–337) and was still a sect treated with suspicion and to bouts of persecution, Christians nonetheless took on the role of nursing plague victims with a readiness and a disregard for their personal safety that is vividly presented in ancient accounts. Historians have long cogitated over the reasons why Christianity became the official Roman religion in AD 380, an event so counter to the prevailing culture that it seems almost to defy explanation. One reason may have been Christian altruism during plagues. We have already referred to the Antonine Plague in the introduction. According to the demographer Lyman Stone, many pagans converted to Christianity because of the readiness of Christians to nurse them during the Antonine Plague, sometimes

---

6. Zwartz, "Book: Dominion by Tom Holland."
7. United Nations, "Universal Declaration of Human Rights."

at the cost of their own lives. Survivors were so impressed by the Christians' valorous love that they saw it as evidence of God's existence and converted.[8]

The same thing happened during the Plague of Cyprian, named after Bishop Cyprian of Carthage (c. AD 210–258) whose sermons described the symptoms.[9] Reckoned by some historians to have been an outbreak of Ebola, it afflicted the Roman Empire from AD 249 to 262.[10] As with the Antonine Plague, this plague triggered an enormous growth of Christianity. Urged on by Cyprian's sermons, Christians came to the aid of the sick. Presented with such an example of selfless, indiscriminate love, people converted to Christianity.[11]

So dedicated were Christians to caring for plague-struck people that Emperor Julian (AD 331–363), a devout pagan, complained bitterly that Christians would even care for sick people who were not Christians, thus winning converts from paganism from among those for whom they cared.[12] So effective were Christians in nursing the sick that the sociologist and demographer Rodney Stark is of the opinion that active Christian communities reduced the death rate by half in the cities where they lived.[13]

The habit of caring for plague victims was not peculiar to ancient Christians; there are excellent examples of this tradition of Christian love continuing into the early modern and modern periods. In 1527, the bubonic plague attacked the people of Wittenberg.[14] Its most famous resident, Martin Luther (1483–1546), refused to leave and stayed to help the sick. He paid an enormous price for this decision because the plague killed his baby daughter Elizabeth (1527–1528).[15] Luther was of the opinion that Christians

8. Stone, "Christianity Has Been Handling Epidemics for 2000 Years."
9. Stone, "Christianity Has Been Handling Epidemics for 2000 Years."
10. Stone, "Christianity Has Been Handling Epidemics for 2000 Years."
11. Stone, "Christianity Has Been Handling Epidemics for 2000 Years."
12. Stone, "Christianity Has Been Handling Epidemics for 2000 Years."
13. Stone, "Christianity Has Been Handling Epidemics for 2000 Years."
14. Stone, "Christianity Has Been Handling Epidemics for 2000 Years."
15. Stone, "Christianity Has Been Handling Epidemics for 2000 Years."

The Practical

with responsibilities of care such as doctors and pastors ought not to leave their posts and be prepared to die at their posts if necessary because of the self-sacrificing example of Christ.[16]

Coming forward in time to the twentieth century, we come across the notable example of the nuns of Philadelphia. When the so-called Spanish Flu arrived in Philadelphia, it struck the city hard, killing seven hundred on 16 October 1918 alone.[17] As the First World War was still being fought, many American nurses were staffing military hospitals and there was a grave shortage of nurses back home. In response, two thousand nuns from across Philadelphia's diocese volunteered to work in the city's hospitals.[18] They cared for people of all ethnicities and creeds, working twelve hours shifts in overcrowded wards.[19] Twenty-three nuns died from the Flu.[20] So impressed was the Mayor of Philadelphia that he declared he had never before seen such self-sacrifice.[21]

The nuns of Philadelphia had the advantage over the ancient Christians of living during a time of better medical understanding and treatments. Germ theory and antiseptics were vital in the war against the Spanish Flu. The nuns had another advantage: They were able to care for their patients in hospitals dedicated to caring for the sick. There is an historical irony here since the nuns had returned to work in the institutions that their ancient and medieval forebears had created, but from which they had been displaced by the professionalization and specialization of medical care.

Indeed, Christians created the first hospitals as a way of helping to prevent the spread of plagues because in their minds not doing what they could to prevent the spread was negligence and ultimately murder.[22] The grand tradition of hospitals created by monks and nuns stretches back to the days of Constantine. These

16. Stone, "Christianity Has Been Handling Epidemics for 2000 Years."
17. Bense, "The Nuns of 1918."
18. Bense, "The Nuns of 1918."
19. Bense, "The Nuns of 1918."
20. Bense, "The Nuns of 1918."
21. Bense, "The Nuns of 1918."
22. Stone, 'Christianity Has Been Handling Epidemics for 2000 Years.'

hospitals existed across the Empire from the Byzantine East to the western shores of the Iberian Peninsula, a heritage of mercy that had no precedent within pagan society.[23] Once Christianity became the official religion of Rome, Christians who were now free of suspicion and persecution were able to organise officially and publicly their charitable works. Certain names merit recognition. When plague struck the city of Edessa, St Ephraim the Syrian (AD 306–373) set up hospitals open to all sufferers.[24] St Basil the Great (AD 329–379) established a hospital in Cappadocia and worked himself in the ward set aside for caring for lepers.[25] The monks at Monte Cassino under the leadership of St Benedict of Nursia (AD 480–547) founded a hospital which the monks staffed themselves.[26] All of these hospitals were opened in the eastern part of the Roman Empire. As women have played a pivotal role in health care historically, it is no surprise that it was a woman who established the first hospital in Rome's western provinces. She was the Christian aristocrat and intellectual St Fabiola (died AD 399) who despite her position of privilege would tour the streets looking for sick people whom she could admit to her hospital.[27] Other examples come to mind. St John Chrysostom (AD 347–407), the patriarch of Constantinople, organised hospitals in that city and established a tradition which lasted for centuries in which rich Christians provided medical assistance to the sick and alms for the poor, the two problems often going hand-in-hand.[28] The Benedictine monks were responsible for setting up two thousand hospitals in medieval Europe.[29] The twelfth century was a high point in the building of hospitals through the efforts of the Knights of St John who for their work came to be known as the Hospitallers. Christians organised not only hospitals but centres of medical training.

23. Bentley Hart, *Atheist Delusions*, 30.
24. Bentley Hart, *Atheist Delusions*, 30.
25. Bentley Hart, *Atheist Delusions*, 30.
26. Bentley Hart, *Atheist Delusions*, 30.
27. Bentley Hart, *Atheist Delusions*, 30.
28. Bentley Hart, *Atheist Delusions*, 30.
29. Bentley Hart, *Atheist Delusions*, 30.

The Hospital of the Holy Spirit, for example, became a teaching hospital, an ancient forerunner of London's St Thomas' Hospital today.[30] Of course, I could go on and give many more examples, but the point has been made. What makes these acts of love so impressive is the fact that working in hospitals exposed the staff to the diseases they were treating. In an age before antibiotics, vaccines, intensive care, and protective clothing, that was a deadly risk. The risk is there today as medical professionals have died of COVID-19 contracted from their workplaces. But as the apostle John (c. 6 AD–c.100 AD) declares: 'There is no fear in love; but perfect love casts out fear . . .' (1 John 4:18). The institution around which nations today are organising their response to COVID-19-the hospital-is an institution created by Christians, perpetuated by Christian civilisation and adopted by civilisations that are not Christian. If our question is where is God in the muddle and pain of a pandemic, then part of the answer is to say that he is there in the form of the hospitals his people inspired many centuries ago and in the form of the people working in them, whether they are Christians or not.

PRESENT DAY CHRISTIAN ACTION

That last point leads me on to the question of what Christians are doing today to mitigate the suffering caused by COVID-19. It is all well and good to point to a glorious tradition of medical care and the arguments of historians about modern science's Christian origins, but what are Christians doing now? Are Christians living up to the high standards set by their forebears in Christ?

To judge the Christian response to the COVID-19 pandemic, it is important to bear in mind that Christians today are in a very different situation to their forebears. In ancient Rome and medieval Europe, there were no national health services. It was Christians who improvized medical care and then established and operated hospitals. With the professionalization of medicine,

---

30. Bentley Hart, *Atheist Delusions*, 30.

Christians still play their part through becoming medical professionals, but it is no longer the exclusive province of the church to create and manage medical facilities. Church buildings have also been closed to prevent COVID-19's transmission and Christians, like the rest of the population, have had to isolate at home. This has limited the institutional and personal efforts of Christians to help.

Yet this has not stopped individuals and groups of Christians from playing their part in this pandemic. From the many examples of Christians playing their part across the world, I shall describe a few examples from my nation, the UK, given by Marcus Jones in his article for Premier Radio's blog where individual Christians have taken the initiative to fill in gaps left by official pandemic aid as a means of showing their and God's love.[31]

Jones describes Matthew Murray, the pastor of Renew Church in Utoxeter, as the 'pizza pastor'. In order to raise funds for local foodbanks by donating from a second income, Murray took on the job of a pizza delivery driver. It also allowed him to keep in touch with his church's members who ordered pizza online. The 'hospital go-between' as Jones names him is David Southall, a hospital chaplain with Worcestershire Acute NHS Trust. As those hospitalised with COVID-19 are left with no access to loved ones, Southall, who is permitted to enter COVID-19 wards whilst wearing protective clothing, volunteered to take written messages from relatives to patients and read them to them. As ambulances were busy ferrying those with serious COVID-19 infections to hospital, a group of volunteers from Ashburton in Devon, which includes Mark Rylands, an assistant bishop in the diocese of Exeter, purchased a black London taxi to transport for free the elderly and vulnerable to hospital for routine appointments who otherwise would have had to have used public transport. Angela Barry from Breightmet in Bolton, with the help of her husband and three sons, set up a stall of free fruit and vegetables outside her house from which anyone could take who needed food during lockdown. All these people are Christians who like their ancient forerunners improvised caring roles during a pandemic.

31. Jones, "Coronavirus: 7 inspiring stories."

The Practical

Of course, Christian organizations and institutions have still managed to find a role too. There are so many examples of this that to discuss them would require that I write another book. However, I should like to present what my own denomination, the Church of England, has been doing during the pandemic. According to an article published online by the Church,[32] it is estimated from a survey of 1,023 Anglican clergy that more than four thousand churches have made great efforts to support their local communities in helping to resolve, or at least mitigate the rising levels of poverty and loneliness caused by the pandemic. Their voluntary help includes the following: food deliveries to the house-bound and those in complete isolation due to medical vulnerability, dog walking, the collection of prescriptions, phone buddies, job hunting support, and helping people to get online. Food provision and pastoral support were by far the most common help that churches rendered. My own parish church has done much through regular donations of large amounts of food to food banks. To the cynic, this activity is a desperate attempt to reverse shrinking congregations. However, the help parish churches give has no strings attached. It is given freely as God's love is.

IN SUMMARY

God is the source of human value which is the foundation of Christian morality that has inspired and continues to inspire Christians to make significant efforts to help the sick. This is not all. Despite what secularists and sceptics say, Christianity has played a major role in the nurture of science and the emergence of modern science, which is central to the war with COVID-19. It is to these startling facts that we turn to in the next chapter.

---

32. The Church of England, "From listening services to food deliveries."

The Scientific

THE NEW ATHEISTS ARE WRONG

THE BEST NATURAL WEAPON that humanity has in the battle against COVID-19 and any other pandemic is modern medical science. Medical scientists have become exceptionally good at studying new viruses and with the vast accumulation of what is already known about viruses generally, they have created new treatments[1] and vaccines for COVID-19[2] very quickly. The New Atheists such as Richard Dawkins and Christopher Hitchens have attempted to convince everyone that modern science is the achievement of secular societies and that Christianity is its enemy. Their narrative is that medieval and early modern Christendom were times of superstition in which the great wisdom of the ancient Greeks was lost and rational inquiry such as science was suppressed. Only when the influence of the church was thrown off by those great cultural watersheds, the Renaissance and the Enlightenment, and scientists were free to do their experiments, was modern science born. This is not only the view of the New Atheists; it is a popular view among secular people and has even affected the thinking of Christians who live within such a secular *milieu*. Such an historical opinion of Christianity's relationship to science is misleading. As I do not have the space in a little book to marshal the many

---

1. "Treatments for COVID-19."
2. "Coronavirus (COVID-19) vaccines."

historical details that refute this simplistic interpretation, I shall present the salient points of Christianity's relationship to science.

THE RELATIONSHIPS BETWEEN RELIGION, CHRISTIANITY AND SCIENCE

Unlike the New Atheists who only see the relationship between religion and science as one of hostility on the part of religion, one of the world's leading historians of science, John Hedley Brooke, describes the relationship as existing in three ways: conflict, complementarity and interrelationship.[3] Conflict there has been, but to reduce the relationship as the New Atheists like to do to one of conflict alone is disastrous. With reference to Christianity, R. K. Merton (1910-2003) advocates what has become known as Merton's Thesis which says that the rise of modern science was assisted by Puritan values of the seventeenth century.[4] In support of Merton, Peter Harrison argues that Protestant methods of interpreting the Bible stimulated scientific inquiry.[5] We will have more to say later in this chapter about the way Christianity provided the fertile cultural soil from which modern science emerged. Therefore, to avoid anticipating a later discussion, I shall stop here. But from this short survey of three leading academics in the study of religion's relationship with science, it is clear that the picture of science and religion's relationship is much more complex than one of simple enmity.

THE BIBLE, THEOLOGY AND SCIENCE

The Bible is a book containing a range of genres such as poetry, history and allegory. It does not have the reputation of a scientific text. Having said this, there are a few perhaps unexpected and significant moments in Scripture where a scientific outlook

---

3. Hedley Brooke, *Science and Religion*, 2, 4–5.
4. Hedley Brooke, *Science and Religion*, 2.
5. Lennox, *God's Undertaker*, 23.

is celebrated. It is in the creation narratives that we see Scripture, theology, and science intersect in that Scripture presents the idea of a beginning of all things, theology adds an insight into where those things came from and science confirms the idea of this particular kind of beginning.

The opening declaration of the Bible states: "In the beginning God . . . created the heavens and the earth" (Gen 1:1). The Bible teaches that the universe had a beginning. This may not seem remarkable to us since other ancient sacred texts[6] describe the beginning of the universe and so too does modern science. However, modern science has not always hypothesized that the universe had a beginning. Indeed, the opinion of leading scientists from the sixteenth century onwards was that the universe had always been there and was infinite in size,[7] an hypothesis derived from Aristotle (384 BC–322 BC).[8] It was a Catholic priest and scientist called Georges Lemaitre (1894–1966) who introduced into science the idea of the universe having a beginning by hypothesizing in 1931 that the universe was the product of the explosion of a primeval atom.[9] Lemaitre died not long after hearing of the discovery of cosmic microwave background radiation which was evidence for the universe having a beginning.

Now some of us might not be impressed with the Bible's accuracy regarding the universe having a beginning. As Dawkins argued in his debate with John Lennox in Alabama in 2007, the writer of Genesis had a fifty-fifty chance of getting it right because either the universe had a beginning, or it did not. The odds were therefore good for guessing correctly.[10] This is true, but there is

---

6. One famous example is *Enūma Eliš* or the Babylonian creation myth which narrates the story of how the god Marduk slays the goddess Tiamat and divides her body in two, making the sky from one half and the earth from the other.

7. Lennox, *God's Undertaker*, 66.

8. Aristotle believed that the earth was at the centre of an eternal universe. Early modern science refuted the belief of the earth as the universe's centre; twentieth century science rebutted the idea of an eternal universe.

9. Lennox, *Gunning for God*, 29.

10. Lennox, *Gunning for God*, 30.

THE SCIENTIFIC

more to the matter than a lucky fifty-fifty guess to which Dawkins likes to reduce it. Ancient theology was teaching by the end of the third century that God had not only created the universe, but had created it out of nothing, or as it is rendered in Latin, *ex nihilo*.[11] Dawkins might retort that again theologians had a fifty-fifty chance of getting it right: either the universe was created out of existing matter, or it was not. However, we have to realise that to hypothesize that the universe had a beginning and that it had come out of nothing was a profound intellectual revolution that challenged the very long-standing Aristotelian orthodoxy that the universe had always existed. To un-think ideas that are very deeply embedded in our culture and advocate radically new ideas is very difficult to do and only the finest minds are capable of it. Take, as an example, the heliocentrism of Nicolaus Copernicus (1473–1543) that overturned slowly the belief that the earth was the fixed centre of the universe. It was not until the twentieth century that the idea of a universe that came out of nothing became orthodoxy. Science had finally caught up with theology. What Dawkins and his New Atheist foot soldiers do not appear to know is that the idea that the universe had a beginning was resisted by some of the best scientists who have ever lived, not because they believed that they had good counter-evidence, but because of their prejudices against the religious idea of creation. Albert Einstein (1879–1955) was suspicious of Lemaitre's idea because it was reminiscent of the Jewish-Christian concept of creation.[12] Sir Arthur Eddington (1882–1944), who was an admirer of Lemaitre's work, nevertheless found the idea of a beginning to the universe to be repugnant[13] which is a value judgement, not a scientific one. In this case, it was atheism or agnosticism that was acting as a break on scientific development in the way that Christianity and religion in general have so often been accused of doing.

Within the description of life in Eden, the garden paradise which God created for humans, we see Adam showing biological

---

11. Lennox, *God's Undertaker*, 66.
12. Lennox, *Gunning for God*, 29.
13. Eddington, "The End of the World," 450.

and taxonomic understanding. According to Genesis 2:19, God creates all the animals out of the ground and then brings them to Adam to see what he will call them. Whatever Adam calls the animals becomes their names. Adam's names probably are the consequence of the characteristics that he observes in each creature. This is a kind of biology. Names are also an essential part of the classification of animals which is known as taxonomy. Adam is therefore thinking empirically which is characteristic of scientific methodology. What is also significant about this episode is that Adam's exercise in biology and taxonomy is not separate from moral questions. Adam finds no comparable helper among all the creatures he meets (v. 20). Adam is learning to appreciate the value of God's animal creation by observing each animal's distinctiveness that calls for and makes possible a name, but also learns the distinctiveness of his humanness for it is only in another human being that the help he needs may come. At the heart of humanness is the capacity for cooperation which though not an exclusive human trait-far from it-it is a remarkable feature of our species.

Within the context of the historical degradation of women as sub-human or a kind of inferior human, this verse is significant. Eve is created as Adam's helper (vv. 21–22). The word helper is vulnerable to misuse to justify the subordinate position into which women have been placed. Eve's role as a helper does not necessarily connote a servile assistant, but can be understood to mean a person who possesses the expertise that another needs. Therefore, when a man consults with his doctor about how best to control his diabetes, the doctor will help the man by drawing on her medical knowledge which he does not have. It is conceivable that Eve has abilities that Adam does not have and her strengths and abilities added to his enable both to care for creation, a task which God delegates to them both equally (1:28).

This inseparability of science from morality which the Genesis creation narratives teach us becomes a more important relationship as science becomes more powerful. The moral question as to whether it is ethical to use gunpowder is a serious one; when the question becomes whether to deploy nuclear missiles, the ethical issues looms far more seriously, for now the matter is one of possible global annihilation. Genesis therefore contains the wise warning to scientists that the power to do something does not mean that that thing ought to be done.

Solomon (c. 990–c. 931 BC), the Israelite king renowned for his great wealth and wisdom (1 Kgs 3:5–13), is distinguished also by his botanical and biological knowledge. According to the writer of 1 Kings, Solomon has great knowledge of trees, plants, animals, birds, insects, and fish (4:33). The writer of 1 Kings prizes Solomon's knowledge because he writes that men from other nations come to listen to Solomon's wisdom (v. 34) and attributes Solomon's knowledge to God (v. 29).

The Bible therefore contains within it the affirmation of the importance of empirical knowledge. Adam and Solomon are held up as examples of this. Aristotle would have been proud. If humans are to supervise and nurture the natural world, it is imperative that they know about it through observation and interaction with it. It is this fascinated desire to know that is the motivational engine of science. It therefore ought to be unsurprising that the earliest scientists in the history of modern science who are most well-known to us, such as Copernicus and Galileo Galilei (1564–1642), were the genius products of Christian universities and heirs to a long tradition of Christian inquiries into mathematics, astronomy, and the physics of motion that can be traced back to the thirteenth century.[14] If a major part of modern science is modern medicine, the discipline that is at the forefront of the fight against COVID-19, it is not implausible to suggest that modern medicine has Christian roots. These are bold claims, particularly within our present intellectual climate in which Christianity continues to be presented as blind obedience to superstitious dogma,[15] but as we will see, this hypothesis has support from historians of science.

---

14. Bentley Hart, *Atheist Delusions*, 58.

15. A recent, prominent example of this vapid stereotyping of Christianity is Freeman's *The Closing of the Western Mind*.

MEDIEVAL SCIENCE

The idea that the Middle Ages were a time of ignorance and superstition because of an irrational, superstitious church, in which the science of the Ancient Greeks was lost until learning was rediscovered by the Renaissance and science was let loose by church-defying heroes such as Galileo remains a popular view of this period. The eighteenth century was in fact the high point of disdain for the medieval period. The influential historian Edward Gibbon (1737–1794), who blamed Christianity for the fall of the Roman Empire, described the Middle Ages as dark in his book *History of the Decline and Fall of the Roman Empire*.[16] Some contemporary scientists have perpetuated this legend. Carl Sagan (1934–1996), who during his life-time became America's best-selling scientist, presented a timeline of science's history in his most popular book *Cosmos*. The timeline is empty between AD 400 and 1500 because according to Sagan, nothing of scientific note happened during those years.[17] That in itself should make us suspicious. The contemporary view of the Middle Ages as a time of brutality is colourfully demonstrated by Mary Wellesley who in her review of Seb Falk's book *The Light Ages*, which challenges the view that the Middle Ages were mad and bad, reminds us that in the film *Pulp Fiction*, Marcellus Wallace tells Zed that he is going to become medieval with his ass. She concludes that what the audience are led to believe will happen is some barbarous punishment, a stereotype of the Middle Ages she says Falk successfully undermines.[18]

The problem critics of Christianity have is that there was no contradiction between belief in God and understanding the world for medieval people.[19] What then did this Christian civilisation achieve? It was monks who translated classical and Arabic scholarly

---

16. Quoted in Falk, *The Light Ages*, 4.
17. Falk, *The Light* Ages, 2–3.
18. Mary Wellesley, "The Light Ages by Seb Falk review."
19. Falk, *The Light Ages*, 5.

The Scientific

works.[20] Universities were established at this time.[21] It was a time also of intense astronomical research, monks inventing mechanical clocks to regulate their devotions and sailors developing new mapping techniques and the magnetic compass.[22] Significantly for mathematics, medieval mathematicians adopted Hindu-Arabic numerals.[23] Alchemists, who foolishly attempted to turn lead into gold, nevertheless developed some procedures still used by modern chemistry.[24] At the heart of this activity was the sponsorship of the great monasteries and the papal monarchy itself.[25]

But what was behind this powerful intellectual and scientific curiosity? Christianity was no impediment to scientific understanding, but we can make a stronger case, namely that Christianity encouraged scientific inquiry because of its view of the created world. It is because medieval theology taught that the universe had been created by a rational God and therefore was ordered and regular that people had faith in the possibility of science as the study of these regularities. A universe that is chaotic and random remains incomprehensible and science is impossible. As the eminent historian of science and mathematician, Sir Alfred North Whitehead (1861–1947), concluded, the faith that science was possible, which led to modern science, was a derivation from medieval theology.[26] Lewis agreed: Pioneers of modern science expected to be able to describe nature in terms of law because they believed in a divine lawmaker.[27]

---

20. Falk, *The Light Ages*, 292.
21. Falk, *The Light Ages*, 292.
22. Falk, *The Light Ages*, 292.
23. Falk, *The Light Ages*, 292.
24. Falk, *The Light Ages*, 292.
25. Falk *The Light Ages*, 293.
26. North Whitehead, *Science and the Modern World*, 19.
27. Cited in Lennox, *God's Undertaker*, 21.

EARLY MODERN SCIENCE

Early modern scientists therefore were, as Isaac Newton (1643–1727) declared himself to be, standing on the shoulders of medieval giants and their giant view of the universe as organised, regular, and therefore capable of being understood. Thus, Francis Bacon (1561–1626), who has the reputation of being the father of modern science, taught that God had created two books: The book of nature and the book of the Bible, and both ought to be studied.[28] His metaphor of a book for nature reveals his view that like a book with its chapters and grammatical rules, the natural world is structured and regular, and so like a book is readable. Galileo has become a hero for anti-theists because his struggle with the Catholic Church has been cast as a struggle between the values of rational science and superstitious Christianity.[29] However, it is often overlooked by Galileo's secular fan club that he was a Catholic whose science was born of his religious conviction.[30] Galileo wrote that God had gifted humanity with their senses and reason and that therefore humans were obliged to use them to gain knowledge.'[31] Johannes Kepler (1571–1630) was of the opinion that the most important aim of investigating the external world was to elucidate the rational order which God had given it and which can be described using mathematics.[32] Newton, whom we have already mentioned, was not an orthodox Christian, but he was a theist who believed there was an intelligent creator who made the universe and who upheld its existence.[33] It is abundantly clear from these examples that rather than being a retardant on scientific enterprise, the Christian faith and Newton's theism were energizers of it. These early modern scientists were continuing the medieval tradition of

---

28. Lennox, *God's Undertaker*, 21.

29. The New Atheist Christopher Hitchens is an enthusiastic promulgator of the Galileo legend. See Hitchens, *God is Not Great*, 255, 260–62, 270.

30. For an understanding of Galileo's Christian beliefs, see Sobel, *Galileo's Daughter*.

31. Lennox, *God's Undertaker*, 21.

32. Morris Kline, *Mathematics*, 31.

33. Lennox. *God's Undertaker*, 8.

regarding the world as a wondrous creation that could be studied. There was no conflict between being religious and scientific in these scientists' minds in the way that the two are seen frequently as separate today. In fact, one can detect in what these scientists say a sense that God has given the universe over to be studied by humans and that to reject that invitation would be a sin against God.

MODERN SCIENCE

So, what about science today? Are there any religious believers within the academic science community, or is science just another name for atheism which the New Atheists would have us believe? In 1997, Edward Larsen and Larry Witham published the result of a survey in which they asked one thousand scientists selected at random whether they believed in a God who answered prayer and in personal immortality. 60 percent of those contacted responded and the results were as follows: 39.6 percent said yes, 45.5 percent said no and 14.9 percent were undecided.[34] The results would have been different if the views of the 40 percent who did not respond were known and if the concept of God presented was simply that of a creator or a divine being rather than one who also answers prayer and makes everlasting life possible. In the case of the less specific notion of a creator or a divine being, the percentage who believe may be higher. Though not a scientist, the philosopher Anthony Flew (1923–2010) is a good example of this way of thinking. After a life of academic writing in favour of atheism, Flew concluded towards the end of his life that there existed a self-sufficient, unchanging, all-powerful, and all-knowing creator Spirit, but that this was a God who had no communion with humanity.[35] However, Flew remained open to the idea that God might one day speak to him.[36]

---

34. Larson and Witham, "Scientists are still keeping the faith," 435–36.
35. Flew and Varghese, *There is a God*, 155.
36. Flew and Varghese, *There is a God*, 155.

What then can be concluded from these results? It is important not to make statistics say what we want them to say. The survey does not warrant the conclusion that atheism is more likely to be true than religious beliefs because the percentage of respondents who reported atheist belief is 5.9 percent higher. We also cannot draw either the conclusion that people are scientists because of their religious and atheist beliefs, or that they are excellent scientists because of those beliefs. What can be ascertained with good reason is that both religious and atheist beliefs are no barriers to a person being an established scientist. In the case of atheism and science, this is not a surprise, but in the light of the fact that modern science today has the reputation of being an atheist project, the fact that there are so many religious believers within the ranks of contemporary science needs to be underscored.

IN SUMMARY

To say that Christianity has played a decisive role in the rise of modern science does not mean therefore Christianity is a true religion and that the Christian God exists. What it does mean is that when attempting to understand COVID-19 from a Christian perspective and when responding to the question of how can God, if he exists, could permit the COVID-19 pandemic, we can go some way to answering that question by pointing to modern medicine. God has not left us defenceless in the face of the virus and Christianity has played its part in establishing modern medical knowledge. However, if I am to press for the existence of God in the first place, the philosophical question of the problem of pain needs to be addressed. This is the next chapter's focus.

The Philosophical

THE PERENNIAL QUESTION AGAIN

I APPROACH THIS CHAPTER with some trepidation. The problem of natural evil, or pain as I have called it, is a vast philosophical subject that that has been examined by theologians and philosophers for centuries. It is a problem not only for Christianity but for Judaism and Islam also. It is one of the great problems of the philosophy of religion. To attempt to write something meaningful about it in the short space I have set myself is very difficult. I do not want to do the subject an injustice. I am also aware that this chapter will feel more objective, detached, and less pastoral than previous chapters. This may not suit everyone, particularly for the many for whom the misery inflicted by COVID-19 and its variants is still raw. However, it is impossible to explore the Covid tragedy without facing the question of whether God exists and whether he is all-powerful, all-knowing, and all-good given the existence of suffering. We have to be pastoral in our attitude, but the comfort and courage we need to face this time of trial will not be able to sustain us if they are grounded on poor or no rational bases.[1]

MODUS TOLLENS

It is possible to respond to the problem of pain indirectly. Rather than explaining how God can co-exist with pain, it is possible to

---

1. Gooding and Lennox, *Suffering Life's Pain*, 96.

argue for God's existence on the basis of other reasons for believing in his existence which are no less powerful than pain and which cumulatively, it is argued, outweigh the force of the argument from pain.

Take the following argument:
Let p=pain exists and q= God does not exist.
If p then q (if there is pain then God does not exist).
p (pain exists).
Therefore, q (therefore God does not exist).[2]

This argument seems watertight. However, by changing the argument structure to *modus tollens*, it is possible to argue that suffering's existence does not prove God's non-existence:

If p then q (if pain exists, God does not exist).

Not q (it is not the case that God does not exist due to the weight of other evidences).

Therefore, not p (therefore it is not the case the existence of pain undermines the argument for God's existence).

These other evidences are the ontological, cosmological, design, moral, and religious arguments.[3] From a Christian perspective, we can also add to the list the historical evidence for Jesus' resurrection.[4]

The success of the above *modus tollens* argument depends on how convincing the 'other evidences' are. Moreover, the argument is a defense of the belief in God in the face of pain in that while it does not explain how God is congruent with pain, it denies the force of the argument that God must be incongruent with pain by appealing to grounds for believing there is a God. Our task, therefore, is to explore ways in which God is congruent with pain. To understand how the Christian God can co-exist with pain, I shall begin by explaining how pain may not be incongruous with God if we consider the sort of world we live in. I shall then explore

---

2. DeWeese, "Solving the Problem of Evil."
3. DeWeese, "Solving the Problem of Evil."
4. For a discussion of why the resurrection is the best explanation for what happened to Jesus, see Habermas and Licona, *The Case for the Resurrection of Jesus*.

The Philosophical

how God is congruous with pain through how he turns all circumstances to the good of those who love him. It is my view that pain has its origins in human free will decisions and not God's. However, I shall defend God's decision to create the world knowing beforehand that it would go wrong through human choice and the view that God is congruous with pain because of love and free will. Finally, I shall examine how humans regard pain as an intruder in their world, thus suggesting that perhaps the world is not meant to be this way, but was created by a God who wanted it to be a place he called very good.

These are Christian arguments, but it ought to be acknowledged for the sake of accuracy that they are not exclusively so. Although I have expressed earlier that my knowledge of how other religions' deal with the problem of pain could be better, I know enough to realise that there are significant crossovers, for example, between Christianity and Islam. Within Islam, there is the beautiful image of Divine Wisdom weaving the threads of pain and suffering into a narrative in which good comes from all miseries.[5] This corresponds with Paul's belief that God works for the good in all circumstances for those who love him (Rom 8:28). There is also the belief that evil and pain are the consequence of human free will and not God,[6] which is a central argument within Christian philosophy.

What is distinctly Christian in my approach to pain is the incarnation, death, and resurrection of Jesus: Events that are held to be historical facts and the expression of God's will only by Christians. It is these events that enable Christians to assert that God has suffered too in the ways we do and that they have created the means of rescue from evil and pain. They are also reasons to believe that God is good, for it is arguable that he is evil, or that he is both good and evil from the existence of good, evil, and pain in the world. This question of God's moral status I shall return to in the conclusion.

---

5. Elshinawy, "Why Do People Suffer?"
6. Elshinawy, "Why Do People Suffer?"

PAIN'S BENEFITS

A case can be made that there is benefit to some kinds of pain. It warns us of impending injury, for instance.[7] So if we are running and we pull a muscle, we will experience pain which causes us to stop running and avoid further injury to the muscle. People derive satisfaction from having overcome pain whilst striving for a difficult, cherished goal. In his contribution to a book on the leadership skills of Britain's elite special forces, Antony 'Ant' Middleton writes that during jungle training, his feet had become badly blistered and he was in agony. Despite this, he went on to pass the 'Survive, Evade, Resist, Extract' stage of training and was proud of overcoming his pain to graduate into the Special Boat Services.[8] By going through difficult times and coming out of rock-bottom, despite the pain involved, we come to know ourselves truly and we develop character.[9] In these instances, people bring good out of suffering by achieving good goals by enduring suffering until it ends. God acts like this too: As Romans 8:28 says, 'all things work together for good for those who love God, who are called according to his purpose.' 'All things' must include pain as pain is something. Such is the way of God and us in a world that has pain.

I think that there is a possibility that there was no pain in the Garden of Eden. I suppose this because the City of God, the New Jerusalem, which is also paradise, is described in Revelation 21:3-4 as follows: '... and God himself will be with them; he will wipe every tear from their eyes. Death will be no more; mourning and crying and pain will be no more...' I am also open to the possibility that Eden and the New Jerusalem are not exact parallels (clearly one was a garden and the other is a city) and therefore some limited instances of pain existed in the Garden from which a greater good always emerged. When God tells Eve the consequences of her having sinned, he says that he will 'greatly increase' her 'pangs in childbearing' (Gen 3:16) which suggests that there was some

---

7. Lennox, *Where is God in a Coronavirus World?*, 17.
8. Middleton *et al*, *SAS Who Dares Wins*, 33-34.
9. Lennox, *Where is God in a Coronavirus World?*, 18.

pain associated with childbirth in Eden. Whether or not there was pain in Eden and to what extent, the question still remains: Why did God allow pain (if there was no pain in Eden) or so much pain into his creation (if there was limited pain in Eden) and why does he continue to permit it?

THE ORIGIN OF PAIN

For pain or more pain to enter what God has created requires the action of someone who has the power to let it in and through whose actions God's creation can be changed. Perhaps it should not therefore surprise us, though it ought to discomfort us greatly, to learn that it is humans who are responsible. According to Romans 5:12, sin enters the world through Adam's disobedience to God, death enters through sin and death spreads to all people because all sin. With death comes pain for the causes of death are frequently painful and grief is always painful. How then do Adam and Eve disobey?

Commonly in British culture, Adam and Eve's wrongdoing is portrayed as eating an apple they were told by God not to eat. No one knows what kind of fruit it is they eat and the idea that it is an apple comes from the fact that the apple is indigenous to Britain. The pair's wrongdoing seems trivial when presented like this. It seems no more serious than what was known when I was a child as 'scrumping' which refers to children stealing apples from other people's gardens. Yet Adam and Eve do not eat an apple pilfered from someone's garden but fruit from the tree of the knowledge of good and evil. Eve's motivation to eat the fruit comes from her desire to be like God and know the difference between good and evil (Gen 3:4–7). She gives some of the fruit to Adam who eats it also (v.6). The Bible does not explain why he does so, but presumably his motivation is the same as Eve's. Their sin which takes the outward form of eating what is prohibited to them is the disposition of lawlessness (1 John 3:4). This is an attitude of independence in which humans follow their own will in defiance of God and his will.[10] To our individualistic culture, this sounds a good thing. Why should anyone submit without reservation to another's will? We have no room for a full discussion of the relationship between God's will and human free will. The point that can be made is that submission to God is not complete submission since there is much room for human freedom within the context of God's sovereignty.

God's will is sovereign in that there are those things that God wills over which he will not compromise and which will come to pass. It was God's will for the Son of God to be born as a human being, die for sin and then rise from the dead. No power or authority could have prevented that from happening. It is God's will that Jesus returns and judges humanity. Again, nothing and no one can prevent this from taking place.

To the New Atheists and their devotees, this means that God is a dictator, something that makes them glad there is no evidence that God exists and on which they base their denunciation of Christian morality. On the contrary, human free will fits perfectly well with God's sovereignty. Though God's provision of salvation and judgement are divinely determined, humans are free to reject salvation and how they will be judged is determined by their moral choices. We are therefore truly free, not to thwart God's universal, sovereign plan, but to thwart it regarding ourselves, though we will also suffer the consequences, which is separation from God if we choose that path.

From my experience as a Christian, I am also aware of how God expresses no will. To give a very simple example, I do not consider God's will when I choose to wear a blue or a purple shirt because I am very sure that God's has no express will in this matter. This does not mean that God cannot express his will regarding my choice, but as far as I am aware, he never has.

Such a freedom might seem trivial, so here is a more serious example. Some years ago, I took up piano lessons. I could have gone back to playing the clarinet, but instead I chose the piano. In my choice of instrument, God played no part. God did not tell me to take up piano lessons or return to the clarinet; as far as I

---

10. Gooding and Lennox, *Suffering Life's Pain*, 124.

can tell it was my decision. Frederic Chopin (1810–1849) is one of my favourite composers for the piano. That I greatly enjoy his compositions is my choice, not something God has willed of me. I learned a simplified version of one of Chopin's Nocturnes: *Nocturne Op. 9 No. 2*. I could have learned *Clair de Lune* by Claude Debussy (1862–1918), but I chose Chopin. How I interpreted the piece through the way I played it was also my choice. All of these decisions were never trivial for me. They were important decisions in which I creatively made choices without God instructing me in any way.

However, on the horizon of human free will is always God's will. My choice to learn piano and play something akin to Chopin's famous *Nocturne* was an expression of my sovereignty as a free will human being. If on the other hand I had chosen to learn to play and sing pop songs with violent and sexually explicit lyrics, these actions would have transgressed God's will that we do not use foul language (Eph 4:29).

Through their sin, Adam and Eve bring death into the world (Rom 5:12). This is not only spiritual death in that their relationship with God is now fractured but also physical death. Everyone now dies because they are sons of Adam and daughters of Eve, even if they are born again and are true followers of Jesus, for though Jesus has defeated death on the cross, death has not yet been cast into the Lake of Fire (Rev 20:14). It is important to note that nowhere in Scripture are Adam and Eve described as possessing immortality inherently.[11] To live forever, Adam and Eve would have to eat regularly from the Tree of Life.[12] What sort of sustenance God provides through this Tree the Bible does not say.[13] But when Adam and Eve are expelled from Eden for their sin, they no longer can eat from the Tree and the natural processes of ageing and eventual death take over.[14]

---

11. Gooding and Lennox, *Suffering Life's Pain*, 129.
12. Gooding and Lennox, *Suffering Life's Pain*, 129.
13. Gooding and Lennox, *Suffering Life's Pain*, 129.
14. Gooding and Lennox, *Suffering Life's Pain*, 129.

Adam and Eve's disobedience not only affects humanity but the whole of the natural order. Humanity was created to be the managers and developers of the earth whilst living in fellowship with God.[15] After Adam and Eve's disobedience and the continued disobedience of all human beings since, the world has been in the hands of very imperfect human masters who are prone to self-centredness and averse to working with and doing God's will.[16] The consequence for the earth is that it is "subjected to futility" (Romans 8:20.) As humans ever since have not played their part wholly correctly in its supervision, the natural world cannot fulfil the purpose of its existence.[17] It too is subject to the power of death, for it is suffering the "bondage to decay" (v. 21). Creatures and other living entities in the natural world therefore die too. Within the natural world are forces of death that are deadly such as predators, bacteria, and as we are now being reminded, viruses. Our death's causes lurk externally as well as internally and we have brought this on ourselves and upon the natural world.

FREE WILL AND LOVE

Could God not have engineered the situation so that no person transgressed his law? The answer to this question is yes, he could have, but it would have meant creating us in a radically different way. It would have meant that God either took away our free will and ensured that we only ever behaved in accordance with his moral standards, or gave us free will, but obstructed our choices when we chose wrongfully, which in essence is not really having true free will. In the first case, what would make matters intolerable would be if we had no capacity to choose, but were conscious of our behaviour being determined. It is conceivable that we could have been made by God to be happily conscious of our behaviour being determined. Nonetheless, none of these alternatives strike

---

15. Gooding and Lennox, *Suffering Life's Pain*, 130
16. Gooding and Lennox, *Suffering Life's Pain*, 129.
17. Cranfield, *Epistle to the Romans*, Vol. 1, 416.

The Philosophical

me as desirable. The principle reason for my saying this is found in a statement made by the atheist Jean-Paul Sartre (1905–1980) who has much to say about personal freedom.

In his *magnum opus*, *Being and Nothingness*, Sartre writes that a lover does not want the beloved to be enslaved or to be a robot whose love is psychologically determined.[18] Put another way, the lover wishes to be loved in return by the beloved which is an act of free will on the beloved's part. To draw a forced love, which is no love at all, does not satisfy the lover and is humiliating. The lover believes s/he is loveable and therefore deserves to be chosen freely by the beloved.

It is easy to see why God has endowed humans with free will. God who is love (1 John 4:8) does not wish to force love from us, for that would not be loving and what we gave him back would not be love anyway. He does not want robots programmed through determinism to 'love' him as he is sublimely worthy of our love and therefore deserves to be loved which to be love can only be given freely. The free will he has given us enables us to love him and each other. God seeks our love not because he needs it as he is wholly self-sufficient, but because he enjoys our love and wants us to benefit from the love relationship we can have with him.

Not only is free will the source of love in that it makes love possible because love cannot by definition be forced from someone, it is also an indispensable reason for why someone might be loved. When X loves Y, s/he loves what is uniquely Y. X finds Y in his/her 'Y-ness' lovable. Free will is part of the essence of our individuality. (We are also individuals for reasons that we cannot help, such as our genetic inheritance.) It is at the heart of our personal individuality in that it makes us unique people. Our decisions may be the same, but the way we carry them out and what we make of those decisions' consequences are specifically us and make us specifically who we are. Take, for example, A and B who choose to study English Literature at the same university. Both are diligent students and progress on to do a master's degree and then a doctorate. Their decisions look the same, but they differ also

---

18. Gooding and Lennox, *Suffering Life's Pain*, 53.

significantly. A chooses to specialise in Anglo-Saxon poetry and B decides to specialise in Christina Rossetti's poetry. Once she has graduated with her doctorate, A takes a job in publishing and remains happily single for the rest of her life. One day, C meets B and falls in love with her, partly because of her intellectuality and great knowledge of literature. He likes the way she speaks about poetry as he knows little about it as his degree was in sociology. It was B's free decision to become an academic and her choice of literature as her field that is one of the reasons why C loves her. There is an 'I' written all over B. If B reciprocates C's love, it is because C has qualities that she finds lovable that are a unique manifestation of him. He too is an I. What therefore unfolds within a relationship includes what each person is through freely chosen decisions.

The means by which we love and are loved is free will therefore, but the price of free will is the wrong that people commit because they are free to do it. Whenever people do wrong, they are being unloving: They are putting their freedom of choice to work for the opposite of what it was intended for. The wrong people do is, as I have said before, evil, but it is the evil that Adam and Eve committed and which humans have committed ever since that has also led to pain. COVID-19 was first identified in Wuhan in China and zoonosis probably accounts for its existence. However, its ultimate source lies in a corrupted natural world that is characterised by decay because of its human masters' sin. This is a good reason not to think that COVID-19 is God's judgement. The pandemic can be traced back to human failing whose consequences God has allowed, but which he has not directly inflicted.

SHOULD GOD HAVE CREATED IN THE FIRST PLACE?

The objection we now face is that if the option of creating humans as robots is not one for a God of love, ought God not to have created the world and its rebellious humans in the first place, for he would have foreseen the pain that lay ahead by creating free willed humans? This is a powerful objection for surely a God who is perfectly loving would not wish to create such a world. It is an issue not of whether existence is preferable to non-existence but whether a certain kind of existence which is characterised in the way ours is by pain is preferable to non-existence. Surely there is truth in how Wilfred Owen (1893–1918) in his Great War poem *Futility* questions the value of existence in the face of the enormous magnitude of death and suffering caused by the fighting by calling prehistoric sunbeams idiotic for bringing life out of the primordial clay in the first place?[19]

I have two responses to this objection: the first regards human behaviour and the second regards God's love.

Let us take the case of Owen and his fellow soldiers. Owen did not survive the First World War as he was killed a week before the armistice was declared on 11 November 1918. If he had lived, he would have, like the rest of his comrades, returned home and sought to give his life a purpose, despite the appalling suffering he had seen and endured. It might be objected that this demonstrates nothing for such a man can live out the rest of his life still convinced that life is not worth it, but refuses suicide and goes on living for the sake of those who love him. That can often be the case. What is important to remember is that many of those former soldiers went on to *choose* to have children with their wives, despite the suffering they had known. It is one thing to go on living oneself with thoughts of how worthless life is because of its suffering; to bring others into this world is a sign that there is something to human life that is worth it and made more worthwhile if we share the opportunity of it with our offspring.

Indeed, I am always struck by the joy that mothers of new born babies evince. They are elated that their labor is over and their child has been delivered safely. Their delight also is at the fact that they have a son or daughter and can share each other's lives. Whatever may befall that child in life, the fact that s/he is here is a cause of great celebration which often begins when the mother discovers she is pregnant. From that perspective, life with its joys and sufferings is worth it after all.

---

19. Owen, "Futility."

Our social structures continue to affirm that life, despite its sufferings, is worth it. We educate our children to be able to have the employment they want. We maintain medical services to improve, prolong and save lives. Our social services exist to reduce and resolve individual and familial problems. The welfare state gives people the basic minimum so that they have at least some dignity. Charities raise money to improve people's lives. The rescue services launch their lifeboats and helicopters to save people from the sea, the wilderness, and mountain ranges. Overseas aid is given to help keep alive those in dire need in other parts of the world. Suicide is regarded as a tragedy (although some cultures have advocated suicide in certain conditions such as defeat in battle and impending captivity). Premature death strikes us as very unfair. It pleases us that someone has lived a long life; we do not mourn that they were in this world for so long. A faith in the desirability of existence even in a world such as ours therefore seems to be the default position.

GOD'S LOVE MAKES IT WORTH IT

The best reason for creating humanity with free will despite the enormous suffering that results is the opportunity to know God's perfect and everlasting love. I would venture that knowing God's love forever in the kingdom he has prepared for those who love him is worth the pain that we experience in this temporal life. This is difficult to accept by those in the throes of pain and those who do not know God's love and doubt he is loving any way because of their pain. Those who know God's love do understand this principle well.

What then is God's love like that makes it worth the suffering that is caused by our free will that enables us to love God? The love of God is perfect. It is a love that forever gives of itself to others.[20] It is a love that is perfectly morally good for God is the final, absolute

---

20. Grudem, *Systematic Theology*, 198.

standard of the good.[21] It is therefore a love that will always give and do the best for the ones God loves for God is faithful.[22] It is a love that carries no conditions or 'strings attached' for God, being wholly self-sufficient, does not need our love in the way that we humans need love. He is loving towards us simply because he is love.[23] If there is an agenda behind God's love it is solely our good and not his, for he needs no good in return. This agenda is what is best for us and the creation of which we are part: That is, that we humans are reconciled to God despite our sin and that the whole cosmos functions harmoniously. This state we might call the peace of God which elicits the praise of God's children and the whole of the natural world.[24] Yet God responds to our love, for if he did not, our relationship to his love would not be a relationship at all, for an essential part of loving someone is to enjoy their enjoyment of our love. Therefore, Scripture clearly states that God rejoices over those who love him (Isa 62:5).

FOUR ALTERNATIVES THAT GOD COULD HAVE CHOSEN

Yet there are four ways in which God could have done things differently regarding humanity and pain whilst preserving free will. If human sin, freely chosen, is the cause of the pain that we suffer, could God therefore have:

1. given humans free will, but not the responsibility for supervising the natural order?
2. Endowed humans with supervision of the natural order, but intervened to prevent the fall of the natural world into pain?

---

21. Grudem, *Systematic Theology*, 197.
22. Grudem, *Systematic Theology*, 195.
23. Williams, *Tokens of Trust*, 12–13.
24. Williams, *Tokens of Trust*, 8.

3. If the natural order is allowed to fall into pain, could God not intervene each time the natural order threatens to cause pain?
4. If there is a measure of utility to the occurrence of pain, could God not prevent the worst pains?

These are serious questions and not easily answered for they ask us to enter truly the mind of God. However, there are some things that can be said in response to make these mysteries lesser mysteries and give ourselves reasonable grounds for our belief in God. What follows are sketches of possible explanations and fragile theodicies that suggest.

In response to (1), God made humans in his image because he seeks a love relationship with human beings. Such a relationship requires some common ground between God and people. The point of contact between God and humanity is in humanity's position between God and creation. Humans are made from the dust from which all creation is made, but also are spirit by which they can know God in deeper, more profound ways than the rest of creation. God calls his people his children in the sense that he asks them to trust him as children trust their parents, but he does not want them to be immature in the sense that they avoid responsibility. Having the chance to be co-regents with God over creation provides that opportunity which is consistent with human dignity.

Part of loving God is to love what he loves, for what he loves deserves to be loved because he, who is perfect love, loves it. We have a choice to love what God loves or not. This means we can choose to love creation or not. Through our frequent decisions not to love God (among those moments when we choose to), we may not be choosing to love creation through obedient co-supervision of it with God. Creation therefore is troubled by this disrupted relationship and this manifests in forces that cause pain. I have long theorised that the creation-shaping force of natural selection with all the pain that accompanies it is a consequence of fallen nature. Under the godly supervision of humanity, the principle of the natural world would be ordered flourishing; in a fallen world where death is ever present, the focus is on survival, hence species' traits are selected for on that basis, rather than chosen through a joyful creativity in which God, humanity, and the natural world participate.

If God then has charged people with responsibility for the supervision of earth, why then not (2)? This is a question of whether it is right to give responsibility, but erase permanently the painful consequences of that responsibility's misuse. My response to this to some extent also is a response to (3). Unless humans possess free will, they can be loved by God, but they cannot love God in return, which denies them a relationship of love with him which is the greatest good humanity can know. Freedom means the capacity to make faulty and evil choices with real consequences. Unless consequences, good or ill, do not follow on from our decisions, we cannot say we are truly free, for our decisions are informed by the consequence that we desire. In addition, what motivation would there be for us to be morally good if our actions did not issue consequences? We might still have the motivation to have good motives and thoughts when there is no chance of our enacting them, but what follows on from our actions is an important part of our moral thinking. I know that if I were unfaithful to my wife, it would cause her significant pain, hence, for this and many other reasons, my determination to remain faithful.

As for (4), it is potentially an incoherent argument. Let us imagine that pain can be categorised according to its intensity, duration, and extent in time and space in ten levels with ten being those pains that are the greatest in intensity, duration, and extent and level one pains are the least in these categories. This notion of levels is problematic since it raises question as to whether a pain that is long in duration and wide in extent but mild in intensity is worse than a pain that is unbearably intense, but which afflicts far fewer people and lasts for much less time. I do not have an answer to that question. However, for the sake of argument we are assuming that pains can be ranked in this way. Pain in level ten would be of the highest intensity, duration, and extent such as pandemics that kill millions and other phenomena such as starvation to death caused by earthquakes. Pain in level one could be of very limited intensity, duration, and extent such as very small paper cuts to the skin.

If God prevented level ten pains, it would of course alleviate and prevent an enormous amount of suffering. However, those people suffering level nine pains would of course demand that those pains are stopped and prevented. If God acceded to this, then those suffering level eight pains would ask for the same for their pains and so the demands would go on until only level one pains were left. Those suffering these would have an excellent case for those pains to be removed and prevented. And why stop there? All evil and the suffering it causes would also have to be abolished and prevented. We are now in a situation where there are no painful consequences of any of human behaviour which as we concluded earlier would undermine human moral motivation.

It is essential that we do not think that God never intervenes at all. In the next chapter, we will examine God's rescue 'package' which is an extraordinary level of intervention in our world on our and creation's behalf and which will last forever. God intervenes in ways that are consistent with his sovereignty, but which leave significant consequences of human choices intact. One way God intervenes is in response to prayer. Many people can testify that prayer to God has led to his involvement in their situation in a miraculous way, turning it around to their advantage, reducing the suffering, or stopping the pain altogether. Prayer therefore is God acting on our behalf after we have freely chosen to ask him to do so because he wishes to and because he is able.[25] It is conceivable that God intervenes in other ways that we are not aware of for the scale and complexity of his intervention is beyond our horizons of understanding.[26]

---

25. Dirckx, *Why?*, 62.
26.. Dirckx, *Why?*, 62.

THE PHILOSOPHICAL

PAIN THE INTRUDER

This sense of pain as something that is an intruder into our existence is worthy of note. It is not synonymous with complaining about our pain as we may accept that it is part of the order of things whilst crying out in agony. What we do is also resent pain as something that is alien. Our cry is at the pain of our and others' suffering, but it is also the cry of incredulity that this is happening at all! When we help people who are in pain, we may well do it acknowledging that pain is inevitable. But we also do it because we have a sense that pain ought not to happen. In fact, our response to pain is not only to alleviate it, but also to prevent it, not only because it is painful, but because it ought not to be. For the most part we are not like Dawkins who in a moment of atheist bravado writes that the universe consists of matter subject to physical forces and therefore is wholly indifferent to human consciousness, well-being and justice.[27]

If this is how the universe is, then we and all sentient creatures are working against the grain of our existence because we do not want it to be this way. We humans want there to be justice, not only for us, but also for other creatures who can feel pain. We seek purposes, and if we cannot see one, then as Albert Camus (1930–1960) declares, we create them as a kind of revolt against the meaninglessness that threatens to overwhelm us.[28] We talk in terms of good and evil and really mean it. We marvel at DNA and yet when we fall in love we fall in love with persons rather than DNA transmitters. Dawkins himself does not really want the universe to be the way he describes it. His recent, terrifying experience of a 'road rage' attack on his car by an incensed cyclist wielding a heavy security lock reveals that he is a man who wants justice in a universe that he has declared has none because he tweeted for witnesses of this attack to contact the police.[29] If we consider pain

---

27. Dawkins, *River Out of Eden*, 133.
28. Simpson, "Albert Camus (1913–1960)."
29. BBC, 'Richard Dawkins' car "attacked by cyclist" in Oxford.'

to be an interloper in our universe, something that is absurd[30] at best and horrifying at worst, a feeling that is absolute in us, could it not be the case that the universe was never meant to be a place of merciless indifference after all? Perhaps our suspicions and our desires that it ought not to be this way is because it was meant to be something other than what it is, which is how it was as God created it at the beginning.

IN SUMMARY

In this chapter, I have ministered to minds. I have presented reasons for why I think that a good God such as the Christian God is congruent with pain's existence. It is not only the mind that needs satisfaction regarding pain; the heart does also. I must now turn my attention to ministering to hearts. The next chapter therefore adopts a pastoral approach that seeks not to explain, though explanations are as important, but to comfort and provide hope through an empathetic approach that finds resolution in the Christian Gospel.

---

30. Albert Camus presents the absurdity of our desire for order and meaning juxtaposed with a silent uncaring universe. The suffering that arises from this juxtaposition is absurd also. He rejects religion as a solution because it is a conjuring trick that gives the illusion that there is no absurd contradiction. See Simpson, 'Albert Camus (1913–1960).'

The Pastoral

INSIDE PAIN

SO FAR, I MAY have given the impression that the suffering caused by COVID-19 and the problems it causes for those who believe, like Christians, that God is all-good, all-powerful, and all-knowing can be tidily explained with historical, moral and philosophical arguments. I hope that is not the case. If it is, this chapter suddenly takes on great importance. Previous chapters have looked at the problem of suffering from an external perspective: there is a problem and what means can be used by God-believers to mitigate the problem so that they do not lose their faith and can be confident when speaking with agnostics and atheists about the problem? Such analysis is important so that Christians can give reasons for the hope that is within them (1 Pet 3:15). However, it is as important to explore the problem of suffering from inside by asking what does it feel like to suffer pain? Suffering is an abstract problem viewed from the outside, but by looking at the problem from the inside we can be remarkably honest about it and admit where the loose ends are that cannot be neatly tied into philosophical arguments and therefore demonstrate a true, empathetic understanding that for many will be more convincing than explanations. For the purpose of this chapter, I have restricted the discussion to one of the greatest pains caused by the pandemic-that of grief. I have chosen grief also because I have known and continue to know its pain, though I admit that COVID-19 has not yet caused me grief.

WHAT IS GRIEF?

In chapter one I referred to Lewis' writing about the grief he endured after the death of Davidman. Lewis is arrestingly honest about his suffering and there are points in his writing where he seems on the verge of giving up his Christianity. He begins by describing grief in visceral terms: That it feels like fear in that it produces the same bodily sensations such as the fluttering of the stomach and restlessness.[1] At first, I thought I knew what Lewis meant. Losing someone to death reminds you that their fate inevitably will be yours also. This is true the older we get. I think that one definition of maturity is the acceptance of the fact that death is not something that happens only to others, but that it will happen to us also. This realisation came home to me once I reached my fiftieth birthday. Life looks much shorter and fragile now than it did when I was seventeen and at my happiest. My father died at the age of fifty-four and at the time of writing I am less than two years away from that age myself. The notion of death that weighed very lightly on me as a teenager is not so much taking shape as I do not know how and when I shall die, but the weight of the thought of death has become heavier. I can feel death's presence in my bones.

I do not think, however, that what I have said about fear above is the kind of fear Lewis meant. The fear I have described above is all about me and grief cannot be all about me, though in part it is, for it is about another person dear to me who has died. The fear caused by grief for many people is not knowing where their loved ones have gone and whether they will ever see them again. Materialists who think that we are no more than our material parts know where their loved ones are: They are, for instance, being stored in a mortuary awaiting burial or cremation. The dualists among us who believe in a soul or spirit have the question of where that soul or spirit now is. At my step-father's funeral, the woman who led the service did so with great tact and dignity, but there was one thing in her script that appalled me: She referred to Mike as being 'wherever he is now'. I understand why she said this as the

---

1. Lewis, *A Grief Observed*, 5.

funeral service my mother chose was not a Christian one, despite my step-father having a Christian faith, and therefore the question of what had happened to Mike was left open for each one of us to answer for ourselves. I am a Christian and I wanted to shout, "No, you are wrong! He is with Jesus!" If you asked me what I meant by that, I could give you some answers gleaned from the glimpses that we have of the afterlife in Scripture, but I could not go into detail because there is an awful lot I do not know. In fact, no one knows much about the post-mortem state that is an intermediary between death and the full coming of the kingdom of God.

WHERE ARE THE DEAD NOW?

Answers to the question of where the dead are if we believe that we survive our deaths tend to be euphemistic and comical: If the deceased is a school teacher, we might say s/he has gone to the great staffroom in the sky. We also sometimes say that s/he is watching us from above.

How far do we take these ideas seriously? I think some do, though what constitutes the great staffroom in the sky and the action of watching from above is hard to understand. How can a disembodied soul sit in an armchair in an everlasting staffroom? How can a disembodied soul see things when his/her eyes are decomposed, or burned up? We say these things and then pass on to other matters as if too much inspection of them might reveal that they are too vague to make much sense. Yet I would not want to challenge someone raw with grief over making statements like this. What if s/he does believe that his/her great uncle Tomisin who worked as a teacher for forty years is now in the great staffroom in the sky? What if s/he does mean that great uncle Tomisin somehow has retained his sight? In his/her grief, that might be all s/he has to keep going. In moments like this, philosophical reasoning might have the effect of adding salt to a wound. It is best to wait before suggesting other ways of seeing this.

MORE ABOUT GRIEF

Grief, of course, is more than fear, a fact that Lewis knew very well. Death is the interruption of our love for someone. Death is as far as I can see one of the most frequently personified natural phenomena, for when someone dies, it feels as if s/he has been stolen from us. Someone has done this to us! Dr Death does not care if great uncle Tomisin was someone you loved much; Dr Death will take him away regardless. Grief is therefore a kind of shock at the fact that love cannot prevail over death when loving someone feels as if it can go on forever. It is a form of shock also in that death confirms the loved one's 'otherness'. We loved him/her and s/he loved us back and there was a sense of connection, but now s/he has died, that connection has been severed and we realise that s/he was his/her own person also after all. Death is a public thing, but it is also a private thing for we alone can die our deaths, even if we are surrounded at our deathbed by those who love us. It is also a form of anger at someone being taken from us who was intrinsically valuable and whom we loved as if s/he were everlasting, but who has been taken away. There is anger too over the death of a young one who never had a chance at life. Death is an affront to us and grief is a kind of outrage. Death is also a force beyond our control in that it will happen and that brings us back to Lewis' idea of grief as fear.

AVOIDING THINKING ABOUT DEATH

In the face of death our response might be to avoid thinking about it by absorbing ourselves in life's details. The English poet Philip Larkin (1922–1985) in his last great poem *Aubade* creates a narrator who wakes before dawn and reflects despairingly on his and everyone's inevitable deaths. He finds refuge in the thought of the day's work to come, which distracts from the thought of death.[2]

Work is not the only distraction we deploy, but it is a good one, bringing with it a sense of purpose, of our being needed alive

2. Larkin, "Aubade," *Collected Poems*, 209.

and in the world, of keeping our perspective in front of us rather than looking upwards and downward, which is what the thought of death causes us to do. Yet this victory over death-consciousness is temporary for no matter how hard we dive into our work, we will one day die.

The horror of dying for Larkin is that it robs us of our sensory life and disconnects us permanently from those we love.[3] In asserting this, Larkin is responding to those who say that being dead ought not to be feared since we will not feel it by retorting that that is exactly what we do fear: The loss of the ability to feel. I have always thought that that is an excellent response to those who argue that death ought not to be feared for we will not feel it.

So where is the grief in all of this? It is the grief of the person dying who knows s/he will lose through death the sight, sound, touch, taste, and smell of those s/he loves. It is the grief of the bereaved who will lose the same of the loved one now dying. The living might hold on in some way to those sensory pleasures through photographs, voice recordings, locks of hair, and memories, yet they are not the same as the person standing, or sitting there with us, or walking beside us. They are artefacts of the person which when sensed separately seem to fragment him/her and when synthesised are a simulacrum. What we want is the whole person back with us safe, sound, and happy, and grief is the knowledge that that is what we cannot have. It is death's irreversibility that so appals.

DOES GOD CARE?

The question we have when we are in the grip of grief is: Does God care? There is a story uniquely recorded in John's Gospel (11:1–44) which reveals that God grieves with us and comforts us in ways that are best for us. According to John, two sisters, Mary and Martha, and their brother, Lazarus, are Jesus' friends and disciples and they live in a town called Bethany (v. 1) which was only two miles from Jerusalem (v. 18). Lazarus falls ill (vv. 2–3) and so Mary and

---

3. Larkin, "Aubade," *Collected Poems*, 209.

Martha send a message to Jesus telling him of this and asking for help (v. 3). By the time Jesus and his disciples arrive in Bethany, Lazarus is dead and has been entombed for four days (v. 17). Quite naturally, when Martha meets Jesus, she reproves him for she says, "'Lord, if you had been here, my brother would not have died'" (v. 21). Martha knows that Jesus heals sick people and assumes that he would have done the same for Lazarus his friend. Martha is a follower of Jesus and a devout Jew, and comforts herself with two beliefs. First, she still believes that Jesus can do something in response, but what specifically, she does not know, for she makes the general comment that whatever Jesus asks of God, he will give him (vv. 21–22). Second, she believes that on the last day Lazarus will rise to life in the resurrection (v. 24). Martha's grief is the type that is assuaged by knowing who or what could fix the cause of her grief. She needs hope in the form of a belief, or a person who can help. Jesus gives her precisely that for he reveals himself to her as 'the resurrection and the life' and that whoever believes in him, though s/he may die, will live (vv. 25–26).

Mary's grief is different. Though she also chides Jesus for not being there to heal her brother, her need is to see Jesus suffering alongside her. She wants to know that Jesus feels the same way as she does and that is exactly what happens, for when Jesus is shown Lazarus' tomb, he weeps (v. 35).

There is a debate among theologians and philosophers of religion as to whether God can feel emotions. Is Jesus' divine nature also weeping, or is it only his human nature that weeps outside Lazarus' tomb? This is a complex question, nevertheless, I shall point out some Bible passages that justify why we ought to think that God has emotions.

Scripture describes God as having a range of emotions. As noted earlier, God rejoices (Isa 62:5), he becomes angry with his enemies (Exod 32:10), and he loves forever (Isa 54:8).[4] Most importantly for us, God also grieves (Ps 78:40; Eph 4:30).[5] The most significant difference between God's emotions and humans

---

4. Grudem, *Systematic Theology*, 166.
5. Grudem, *Systematic Theology*, 166.

emotions is that God's emotions are not sinful as often human emotions are: They are always proportionate, justified, and never have less than the right object, intent, and consequence. Our perspective therefore needs to change. Rather than seeing ourselves as reducing God down to our human level by ascribing emotions to him, it is our having emotions that raise us up to the possibility of relationship with God.

The climax of the story is that Jesus raises Lazarus from the dead. I sometimes wonder how frightening it must have been at first for Mary, Martha, and their fellow mourners to see what was once a corpse still bandaged in grave clothes and his face wrapped in a cloth walk out of his tomb! Their initial fear turns quickly to joy and belief in Jesus as they unwrap Lazarus to find that he is not a zombie, but a man alive (11:44).

The significance of this episode is that God feels grief and provides the solution in that he is the solution. We do not have the ability to understand directly how God experiences grief no more than we have the ability to experience directly how other people experience grief or any other emotion. We may behave in the same way as other people when we are grieving, but we have no direct access to the experience of the emotion from their point of view. Our best approximation to knowing how grief feels to God is to observe Jesus' behaviour: He weeps at Lazarus' tomb. God's grief mediated through the person of Jesus is tears. You may have heard that the sacraments such as baptism and marriage are the visible signs of God's invisible grace. Jesus' tears are what is human visibly signing God's invisible grief. God is profoundly moved by our loss of loved ones. He is not inert and distant, comprehending all that happens from his eternal state without reaction; he is not the God of the deists who has made the world and left it to run by itself; he is the God who came into our world, is involved at the deepest level possible and suffers in ways beyond our comprehension. Like Mary, we can take comfort in a God who cares.

If you are like me, you are more of Martha's frame of mind, though we can be both a Mary and a Martha in the face of grief. When someone is in pain my immediate response is to understand why and to find a way of removing the cause of it. I have learned, however, to listen first to what the person wants and needs before I behave in ways I think they want and need. Jesus reveals this perfectly in his conduct: He treats Martha and Mary differently according to their respective needs.

THE RESURRECTION OF JESUS

We have discussed the good reasons to believe that God grieves alongside us. In this pandemic, he is doing the same thing that he does for Mary. Jesus also provides the solution to Mary and Martha's grief by raising Lazarus. He raises Lazarus also to bring himself glory, which he deserves as he is the Son of God (v. 4). God performs miracles out of his great love for people. He also performs them to glorify himself by inciting the praise and worship of people who witness the miracle.

Lazarus' resurrection is a foreshadowing of what is at the heart of the Christian Gospel or Good News, a phrase I think is a serious understatement. Death is not the extinction that horrified Larkin and probably most of us. Instead, it is the resurrection of Jesus that offers all a resurrection to an everlasting life lived in communion with God and devoid of pain and death.

When Jesus died, he could not remain dead, for he is not only a man but also God the Son. His resurrection also was qualitatively different to the resurrections we see in the Gospels. Jesus did not rise back to life and resume living in a body that was subject to pain and death as Lazarus did; rather, he is the 'first fruits' (1 Cor 15:20, 23) of a new type of human life which consists of a body that lives optimally forever.[6] By first fruits is meant that Jesus made it possible for any of us to have this kind of resurrection if we so choose. He is therefore the first person to have this kind of resurrection and those who are saved will also resurrect like him.

This is truly good news, but the path to Jesus' resurrection lies through the salvation he offers. To understand salvation, or

---

6. Grudem, *Bible Doctrine*, 262.

what we can be saved from, we must understand and accept three things:

1. All people are sinners, which means they have failed to live up to God's holy standards in their morality (Rom 3:23).
2. The punishment for breaking God's laws is spiritual death or separation from God forever (6:23).
3. Jesus took the punishment we deserve through his death on the cross (5:8).[7]

It is not enough to believe these things. The devil accepts the truth of the above three statements and yet he is not saved! What is fundamental to a person's salvation is his or her response to Jesus. This means trusting in, or having faith in, Jesus to save us from our sins and turning away from our sins which is called repentance.[8] By the power of the Holy Spirit who lives inside those who are saved from their sins and punishment, we can live changed lives.

RESURRECTION LIFE

What sort of life are we resurrected to? We are promised the forgiveness of sins and everlasting life with God (John 3:16). Revelation 21:1–8 gives us a glimpse of what that life will be like in terms we can understand though not wholly:

> 'Then I saw a new heaven and a new earth; for the first heaven and the first earth had passed away, and the sea was no more. And I saw the holy city, the new Jerusalem, coming down out of heaven from God, prepared as a bride adorned for her husband. And I heard a loud voice from the throne saying,
>
> See, the home of God is among mortals.
> He will dwell with them;
> they will be his peoples,
> and God himself will be with them;

---

7. Grudem, *Bible Doctrine*, 298.
8. Grudem, *Bible Doctrine*, 297.

> he will wipe every tear from their eyes.
> Death will be no more;
> mourning and crying and pain will be no more,
> for the first things have passed away.
>
> And the one who was seated on the throne said, 'See, I am making all things new.' Also he said, 'Write this, for these words are trustworthy and true.' Then he said to me, 'It is done! I am the Alpha and the Omega, the beginning and the end. To the thirsty I will give water as a gift from the spring of the water of life. Those who conquer will inherit these things, and I will be their God and they will be my children. But as for the cowardly, the faithless, the polluted, the murderers, the fornicators, the sorcerers, the idolaters, and all liars, their place will be in the lake that burns with fire and sulfur, which is the second death.'"

Everlasting life will be situated in the New Jerusalem (v. 2). It seems as if followers of Jesus will have some kind of glorious urban life, although it is likely that this is one way of perceiving everlasting life which due to its potential infinity can be viewed from myriad perspectives. Importantly for our discussion, this is a domain where there will be no more death and suffering and where God's people will be with his cherished children (vv. 3–4). Nonetheless, it is a sobering thought that those who remain attached to their sin and refuse Jesus' offer of salvation will be sent to what is known as the lake of fire (v. 8). These are people who are unrepentant and who cannot be allowed to live with God and his people because of their free decision to embrace forever their sin. Their sinful nature would certainly ruin the idyllic conditions with which God wishes to reward the repentant by reintroducing moral evil and pain through their behaviour and attitude.

BECOMING A FOLLOWER OF JESUS

How then does a person who is not a follower of Jesus become one? I became a follower in July 1982 at the age of twelve. A boy who was a year older than me at my school told me the Good News of Jesus' death and resurrection. He was a member of the school's thriving Christian Union which faithfully proclaimed the Gospel to the pupils and students and each morning before school would meet to pray for the school. He gave me a tract or small pamphlet that explained further what he had been saying to me and at the end of it was a prayer which invited me to repent of my sins and follow Jesus. It was made clear to me that salvation is a gift and not something that can be earned since it is impossible for anyone to match the perfect moral standard of God since all have fallen short of it and stand condemned (Romans 3:10). I prayed the prayer and committed myself to Jesus. This meant a life lived in relationship to God through prayer, worship, and meeting with other believers at my school's Christian Union. At the age of sixteen I joined a local church. My following Jesus did not mean stereotypically leaving home and going to a far-off place to be a missionary, which for some people is what Jesus calls them to do, but living a life of faithful obedience where he wants me to be, which was at school, then university, and now in the workplace. It also means faithful obedience to him within the context of my family and other personal relationships.

If you too wish to commit yourself to the love of God through Jesus or wish to recommit yourself, here is a prayer you could say. It is not the prayer I said, but it is something similar:

Lord Jesus,

I confess that I am a sinner and am not living in the way you created me for. Thank you for taking the punishment for my sins by dying on the cross. I fully accept your forgiveness of my sins and now turn away from them so that I can live the new life you wish me to have. As I am now forgiven much, I forgive others who have sinned against me. Thank you also for rising from the dead which is the guarantee that I too, if I die before you return, will be resurrected to everlasting life. I chose to follow you whatever that shape that new life takes. I look forward to the transformation of my character by the Holy Spirit who is now living in me and guiding me.

Amen.

This prayer is only the beginning. It is the first move in a life that has become everlasting and which though it probably will be temporarily interrupted by death and is not immune from suffering, is a life in which nothing can separate us from God's love (8:38–39).

AND THE NATURAL WORLD?

Though this book has focused on human pain, it would be a serious omission to neglect exploring how God will rescue the natural world also. God's rescue package extends to all creation, not only to humans. Human beings suffer every day in immeasurable amounts; so too does the natural world on account of the folly of human sin. Yet what God has in store for the natural world is as much glorious as what he has waiting for his children.

Writing this might surprise many people since Christianity has a poor reputation for its concern for the environment. Surely Christianity with its talk of humans taking dominion over the natural world (Gen 1:26) has encouraged exploitation of it which has resulted in a great amount of pain?[9]

The wording of Genesis 1:26 does require careful handling if it is not to be interpreted as a licence for exploitation. We need to avoid isolating the word dominion from the context of the rest of the verse. The full verse reads:

> "Then God said, 'Let us make humankind in our image, according to our likeness; and let them have dominion over the fish of the sea, and over the birds of the air, and over the cattle, and over all the wild animals of the earth, and over every creeping thing that creeps upon the earth.'"

According to this text, humankind is to have dominion but only in its capacity as image-bearers of God. It is when humans are being god-like that they are qualified to have dominion over

---

9. Runcorn, *Spirituality Workbook*, 162–63.

the world. When people act rationally, are guided by their moral conscience, are obedient to God and are loving, they are capable of exercising the kind of virtuous oversight that causes the natural world to flourish. Though in their sinful condition humans remain made in the image of God, they no longer faithfully bear the image of God to creation. Capable still of care for nature, human behaviour is also marked by exploitation and cruelty and therefore is a source of much pain to sentient creatures.

God's rescue of the natural world is described by Paul like this in Romans 8:18–25:

> "I consider that the sufferings of this present time are not worth comparing with the glory about to be revealed to us. For the creation waits with eager longing for the revealing of the children of God; for the creation was subjected to futility, not of its own will but by the will of the one who subjected it, in hope that the creation itself will be set free from its bondage to decay and will obtain the freedom of the glory of the children of God. We know that the whole creation has been groaning in labor pains until now; and not only the creation, but we ourselves, who have the first fruits of the Spirit, groan inwardly while we wait for adoption, the redemption of our bodies. For in hope we were saved. Now hope that is seen is not hope. For who hopes for what is seen? But if we hope for what we do not see, we wait for it with patience."

The natural order's liberation from decay and death will happen at the moment when the sons of God, a name which refers to all of God's children, both male and female, are revealed in their new nature (vv. 19–21). This glory's revelation will outweigh all the pain that nature has suffered due to human sin (Gen 3:17). The renewal of creation (Rev 21:1) is simultaneous to the freedom of the glory of God's children (Rom 8:17–18). Just as the fall of humanity led to the fall of nature, so the restoration of the redeemed leads to the regeneration of nature.

IN SUMMARY

God extends his rescue to all humanity and to the whole of the natural order. Though we cannot answer completely the problem of pain, we can point to what God has done to provide us and the creation we inhabit with an escape route. Yet, it is more than an escape route. It is the narrow path that leads to living in love with God forever within a regenerated creation. Whether we choose this path or not is our personal decision. It is our freedom that is part of the divine image that we bear. It is also that which determines our future.

Conclusion

A POWERFUL CASE

AS WE HAVE SEEN, a potent case can be made for Christianity in the context of COVID-19. The pandemic is not God's judgement. This is an important conclusion since if it were God's judgement, Christians would be impeded from helping its victims, including the victims in their own communities. As it is a human-made crisis which God has permitted to highlight the need for reform to human attitudes and behaviour, Christians can make a humanitarian response. This they are obliged to do by their own moral framework which gives humans absolute value. Historically, Christians have played a decisively creative role in the treatment of disease and at the moment are playing their part either officially as medical and support staff or through improvised, voluntary services to their neighbourhoods. Christianity too was the cultural soil that nourished science and from which modern science and therefore modern medicine, which is the best weapon against the pandemic, have emerged. The philosophical problem of whether a good God can be congruent with pain was the subject of chapter four. The argument from free will is the principal argument for this congruence. Life remains worth living for the great majority of people and therefore God's decision to create, despite the consequences, is justified. The sublime compensation of loving and being loved by God, made possible by free will, overwhelms the temporary suffering of the world. Finally, we have acknowledged the loose ends of grief and nevertheless have described the Good News of

Christianity which is reconciliation with God and an everlasting, pain-free existence where death and grief are no more. We ended by considering how God's soteriological vision includes the full rescue of the natural world also from pain. Christianity truly has powerful things to say in these times and indeed all times.

THE MYSTERY ABIDES

Despite the above clarities, I have written this book within the context of a powerful sense that what we are dealing with ultimately is a profound mystery. The problems of evil and pain are excellent at reminding us of our predicament that William Alston describes so well: We are firmly circumscribed by our lack of data, the puzzling complexity of many phenomena, the uncertainty as to what is metaphysically possible or necessary, our ignorance of what is fully possible, and our own subjectivities that obscure the truth.[1] What compounds the problems is that what is at the heart of the issue is God who is ultimately mysterious.

However, the writing of this book has been premised on the view that this mystery is not a complete mystery, but one where things are revealed to our understanding, but which we cannot know exhaustively. The eyes of our understanding are closed and yet opened at the same time. We are like Job who in the middle of his pain demands to know why and receives answers from God, but he does not receive complete revelation (Job 38–41). He chooses to trust God nevertheless (chapter 42) and that is the invitation to us all also.

Our response may be determined by our attitude to mystery in this matter. We might be able to tolerate the fact that we do not know all that there is to know about the oceans' depths, for what lies down deep probably will have no effect on us, but if God has something to do with us, we cannot be indifferent to the sort of God that he is. If God is ultimately mysterious, perhaps he is able to appear to be what he is not for reasons understood only

---

1. Alston, "Inductive Argument from Evil," 59–60.

CONCLUSION

by him. Imagine that God is evil and that he has given us free will so that we might hate, for to hate no less than love requires free will. The evil and pain that is the consequence of human free will is exactly what evil God wants. Though love, the greatest good, is the result of free will, evil God endures such love for he prizes hate, the greatest evil, that is manifested by the same free will. If God is evil, then probably there is greater evil and pain than good and pleasure in the world and that if there is an end to such a world, it will be an evil apocalypse. An alternative view is that God is both good and evil which is the cause of there being good, evil, and pain in the world. And if humans are made in God's image, then their Dr Jekyll and Mr Hyde dispositions reflect their creator very well.

I raise this issue at the end of this book, not to undermine my efforts, of course, but to address a final issue. Philosophers like Stephen Law contend that the arguments for God's existence do not give grounds for thinking that God is necessarily good and that the theodicies that explain why God permits evil and pain can be reversed or balanced by reverse and anti-theodicies to justify why an evil God permits goodness and pleasure. This is called the "evil-god challenge."[2]

The best response to this and to the view that God could just as easily be a mixture of good and evil is to point to the incarnation, crucifixion, and resurrection of Jesus as the grounds for believing that God is good. If these are historical facts, and I think they are, then it seems unlikely that God the Son would cross the enormous gulf between God and humanity to endure a life of evil and pain at the hands of others and crucifixion's agony if his love for us is not genuine, whether we are in pain or not. Indeed, it is the deeds of God, born of sublime love, rather than human arguments, that are the best response to pain, something that the great man of God, Job, knew a lot about.

---

2. For a highly readable exposition of his evil god challenge, see Law, "The evil-god challenge," 353–73.

Bibliography

Alston, William. "The Inductive Argument from Evil and the Human Cognitive Condition." *Philosophical Perspectives* 5 (1991) 29–67.
Andersen, K. G., et al. "The proximal origin of SARS-CoV-2." *Natural Medicine* 26 (2020) 450–52. https://doi.org/10.1038/s41591-020-0820-9.
Barnabas Fund. "Over 2,000 Covid deaths amongst pastors and Christian leaders in India and Nepal leave Christians floundering and ministries in danger of collapse." https://barnabasfund.org/news/over-2-000-covid-deaths-amongst-pastors-and-christian-leaders-in-india-a/.
BBC. "Richard Dawkins' car 'attacked by cyclist' in Oxford." https://www.bbc.co.uk/news/uk-england-oxfordshire-59488872.
Bense, Kiley. "We Should All Be More Like the Nuns of 1918: The sisters of Philadelphia were lifesavers during the Spanish flu epidemic. They are an inspiration today." *The New York Times*. https://www.nytimes.com/2020/03/20/opinion/coronavirus-nuns.html.
Bentley Hart, David. *Atheist Delusions: The Christian Revolution and Its Fashionable Enemies*. New Haven: Yale, 2009.
Boice, James Montgomery. *Foundations of the Christian Faith: A Comprehensive & Readable Theology*. Downers Grove, Il.: InterVarsity, 1986.
Bruenig, Elizabeth. "Is the New Atheism Dead? How atheists and the religious are learning to get along." *The New Republic*. https://newrepublic.com/article/123349/new-atheism-dead.
Church of England. "From listening services to food deliveries-churches step up support to local communities during the pandemic." https://www.churchofengland.org/media-and-news/news-releases/listening-services-food-deliveries-churches-step-support-local.
"Coronavirus (COVID-19) vaccines." https://www.nhs.uk/conditions/coronavirus-covid-19/coronavirus-vaccination/coronavirus-vaccine/.
Cranfield, C. E. B. *A Critical and Exegetical Commentary on the Epistle to the Romans*, Vol. I. Edinburgh: T&T Clark, 1975.
Dawkins, Richard. *River Out of Eden*. New York: Basic, 1992.
DeWeese, Garrett. "Solving the Problem of Evil." Lecture, Biola University's Certificate in Apologetics.

BIBLIOGRAPHY

Dirckx, Sharon. *Why? Looking at God, evil & suffering*. Nottingham: Inter-Varsity, 2013.

Eddington, Arthur. "The End of the World: From the Standpoint of Mathematical Physics." *Nature* 127 (1931) 447–53.

Elshinawy, Sh. Mohammad. "Why Do People Suffer? God's Existence & the Problem of Evil." https://yaqeeninstitute.org/read/paper/why-do-people-suffer-gods-existence-the-problem-of-evil#ftnt12.

Falk, Seb. *The Light Ages: A Medieval Journey of Discovery*. London: Penguin, 2020.

Flew, Antony and Varghese, Roy Abraham. *There is a God: How the world's most notorious atheist changed his mind*. New York: HarperCollins, 2007.

Freeman, Charles. *The Closing of the Western Mind: The Rise and Fall of Reason*. New York: Knopf, 2003.

Gooding, David and Lennox, John. *Suffering Life's Pain: Facing the Problems of Moral and Natural Evil*. Belfast: The Myrtlefield Trust, 2019.

Grudem, Wayne. *Bible Doctrine: Essential Teachings of the Christian Faith*, edited by Jeff Purswell, 262, 297–98. Leicester: Inter-Varsity, 1999.

———. *Systematic Theology: An Introduction to Biblical Doctrine*. Leicester and Grand Rapids, MI: Inter-Varsity and Zondervan, 2000.

Habermas, Gary, and Mike Licona. *The Case for the Resurrection*. Grand Rapids, MI.: Kregel, 2004.

Hedley Brooke, John. *Science and Religion: Some Historical Perspectives*. Cambridge: Cambridge University Press, 2014.

Hitchens, Christopher. *God is Not Great: How Religion Poisons Everything*. London: Atlantic, 2007.

Jones, Marcus. "*Coronavirus*: 7 inspiring stories of Christians making a difference." https// https://www.premierchristianity.com/home/coronavirus-7-inspiring-stories-of-christians-making-a-difference/2808.article.

Lamb, Isaac. "The delusions of New Atheism." https://www.tcs.cam.ac.uk/the-delusions-of-new-atheism/.

Larkin, Philip. "Aubade" in Philip Larkin, *Collected Poems*, edited by Anthony Thwaite, 209. Hull and London: Marvell and Faber and Faber, 1988.

Larson, Edward and Witham, Larry. "Scientists are still keeping the faith." *Nature* 386 (1997). https://doi.org/10.1038/386435a0.

Law, Stephen. "The evil-god challenge." *Religious Studies* Vol. 46 Issue 3 (September 2010) 353–73.

Lennox, John C. *God's Undertaker: Has Science Buried Religion?* Oxford: Lion Hudson, 2009.

———. *Gunning for God: Why the New Atheists Are Missing the Target*. Oxford: Lion Hudson, 2011.

———. *Where is God in A Coronavirus World?* Epsom: The Good Book Company, 2020.

Lewis, C. S. *A Grief Observed*. London: Faber and Faber, 1961.

———. *The Problem of Pain*. London: Centenary, 1940.

Bibliography

Merritt, Jonathan. "Some of the Most Visible Christians in America Are Failing the Coronavirus Test: In place of love, they're offering stark self-righteous judgment." https://www.theatlantic.com/ideas/archive/2020/04/christian-cruelty-face-covid-19/610477/.

Middleton, Anthony, et al. *SAS Who Dares Wins: Leadership Secrets from the Special Forces* London: Headline, 2018.

North Whitehead, Alfred. *Science and the Modern World.* London: Macmillan, 1925.

Owen, Wilfred. "Futility." https://www.poetryfoundation.org/poems/57283/futility-56d23aa2d4b57.

Poole, Steven. "The Four Horsemen review - whatever happened to 'New Atheism'?" https://www.theguardian.com/books/2019/jan/31/four-horsemen-review-what-happened-to-new-atheism-dawkins-hitchens.

Porter, Laurence E. "Luke." In *The International Bible Commentary: With the New International Version*, edited by F.F. Bruce, 1210. Grand Rapids, Michigan: Zondervan, 1986.

Reicke, Bo. *The New Testament Era: The World of the Bible from 500 B.C. to A.D. 100.* London: Adam & Charles Black, 1968.

Runcorn, David. *Spirituality Workbook: A Guide for Explorers, Pilgrims and Seekers.* London: SPCK, 2011.

Sagan, Carl. *Cosmos.* New York: Random, 2002.

Simpson, David. "Albert Camus (1913–1960)." *IEP.* https://iep.utm.edu/camus/#SSH5ci

Sobel, Dava. *Galileo's Daughter.* London: Fourth Estate, 1999.

Stone, Lyman. "Christianity Has Been Handling Epidemics for 2000 Years: Practical theology says care, sacrifice, and community are as vital as ever." https://foreignpolicy.com/2020/03/13/christianity-epidemics-2000-years-should-i-still-go-to-church-coronavirus/.

Storrs, Carina. "Endangered Species: Humans Might Have Faced Extinction 1 Million Years Ago: A new approach to probe ancient regions of the genome suggests early human populations were scarce." https://www.scientificamerican.com/article/early-human-population-size-genetic-diversity/.

The Bible: New Revised Standard Version (Oxford: Oxford University Press, 1995).

Tomlin, Graham. "Is the coronavirus a judgement from God? Pestilence tells us more about ourselves than it does about God." https://www.churchtimes.co.uk/articles/2020/1-may/comment/opinion/is-the-coronavirus-a-judgement-from-god.

"Treatments for COVID-19: What helps, what doesn't, and what's in the pipeline." https://www.health.harvard.edu/diseases-and-conditions/treatments-for-covid-19

Wakefield, Lily. "Christian author thinks COVID was God's punishment for sports teams being 'so pro-LGBT.'" https://www.pinknews.co.uk/2021/08/04/william-koenig-lgbt-covid/.

Bibliography

Wellesley, Mary. "The Light Ages by Seb Falk review – banishing the idea of the 'Dark Ages.'" https://www.theguardian.com/books/2020/sep/25/the-light-ages-by-seb-falk-review-banishing-the-idea-of-the-dark-ages.

Williams, Rowan. *Tokens of Trust*. Norwich: Canterbury, 2007.

World Health Organization. "Coronavirus (COVID-19) Dashboard." https://covid19.who.int/.

Wright, N. T. *God and the Pandemic: A Christian Reflection on the Coronavirus and its Aftermath*. London: SPCK, 2020.

United Nations. "Universal Declaration of Human Rights." https://www.un.org/en/about-us/universal-declaration-of-human-rights.

Zwartz, Barney. "Book: Dominion by Tom Holland." https://www.solas-cpc.org/book-dominion-by-tom-holland/.

www.ingramcontent.com/pod-product-compliance
Lightning Source LLC
Chambersburg PA
CBHW071159090426
42736CB00012B/2383